S0-BZP-148

B
CC

ALSO BY ANNIE GILBAR

The Lunch Box Book
The Penny Whistle Party Planner
(with Meredith Brokaw)

THE
ULTIMATE
BREAKFAST
COOKBOOK

Phillip Scully

and

Annie Gilbar

Weidenfeld & Nicolson · New York

Copyright © 1988 by Phillip Scully

All rights reserved. No reproduction of this book in whole
or in part or in any form may be made without written
authorization of the copyright owner.

Published by Weidenfeld & Nicolson, New York
A Division of Wheatland Corporation
10 East 53rd Street
New York, NY 10022

Published in Canada by General Publishing Company, Ltd.

Library of Congress Cataloging-in-Publication Data
Scully, Phillip, 1933–
The ultimate breakfast cookbook
Includes index.
1. Breakfasts. I. Gilbar, Annie. II. Title.
TX733.S38   1987   641.5'2   87-8229
ISBN 1-55584-074-4

Manufactured in the United States of America
Designed by Irving Perkins Associates
First Edition
10 9 8 7 6 5 4 3 2 1

PHOTOGRAPHS BY RONNIE KAUFMAN

To Renée Golden,
my attorney and friend,
for making this possible
—you're the best.

ACKNOWLEDGMENTS

This book would not have been possible without the help of the following people: Renée Golden, Annie Gilbar, Melody, Dan Green, Judie Choate, Ronnie Kaufman, Janet Surmi, and Jane Thompson.

And my special friends and customers: Richard Burton, Neil Diamond, James Garner, John Hurt, Jack Lemmon, Ed McMahon, Jim Mahoney, Dolly Parton, Phil Rosenthal, Topper of Gendarme, and Dave Tebet.

And all my other customers for their encouragement.

—Phillip Scully

CONTENTS

PREFACE
by James Garner

Scully's has long been one of Hollywood's best-kept secrets. There's no fancy front and no sign over the door. And despite its unlisted phone number, you'd better have a reservation or chances are you won't be seated. My first time, even I had to have a referral from another of Scully's established patrons to get in the door. The place is down to earth, warm, and private; perfect for quiet breakfast meetings. But many of us who frequent Scully's—actors and agents as well as a few locals who got lucky by following their noses through the door—are there for only one prime reason: the food.

Phil Scully, a one-of-a-kind, larger-than-life character, complete with his trademark sea captain's cap and healthy-size paunch, cooks up food that will keep you asking for more. The restaurant is his club run according to his rules . . . the first of which is leave your pretensions at home. Chatting with guests, charming them with jokes he picked up from the previous day's customers, Phil Scully gives his friends a good chuckle and gets them to relax so that they may enjoy some of the greatest and most satisfying food to be found anywhere in Los Angeles.

While Scully runs in and out of the kitchen, tempting you with his special creations, Melody—his partner and general overseer of the dining room—gives you the motherly attention that caps off a truly grand meal. The two of them are unbeatable.

Breakfasting at Scully's is one of my favorite indulgences. I practically never miss a chance at the corned beef hash, and his homemade sausage is the best in town. Sometimes I'm tempted by one of his incredible omelets accompanied by homemade marmalade and a variety of homemade breads, or I go for the steak and eggs. It's all great, and lunch is every bit as good and just as filling.

A word of caution for many first-timers who just want a quick bite or only like to pick at their food—Scully's is not for you. Whether you're there for breakfast or lunch, you'll need a healthy appetite. And come to think of it, you might be wise to wear something that's just a little loose around the middle. No one leaves Scully's hungry.

With this wonderful cookbook, now anyone at home can recreate Scully's fabulous food.

THE ULTIMATE BREAKFAST COOKBOOK

INTRODUCTION

I suppose that the ultimate breakfast would be served on a yacht that was resting in the middle of the Mediterranean. There we'd be, my five best friends and I, sitting at a round table set with the finest linens; Rosenthal china in the Royal pattern, of course; Tiffany's Rose Petal silver; the Czar's crystal goblets from Baccarat; with *phaleonopsis* orchids at each plate. The sun would be shining; the morning air warm and relaxing. And the food would be glorious—thinly sliced oranges soaked in Courvoisier would sit by bowls of fresh raspberries in cream; a light, fluffy omelet with potatoes and caviar would be garnished with thin slices of fresh tomatoes and slivers of chives. The smell of freshly baked black bread would fill the air, accompanying the aroma of the coffee brewing by our side. One goblet would be filled with just-squeezed orange juice; the other with champagne. What a glorious beginning to what would have to be a perfect day!

On the other hand, the perfect breakfast would be served in bed. My tray, covered with Irish linen, would be filled with my favorite delights: warm, bursting popovers; mouth-watering orange marmalade containing thick chunks of oranges; paper-thin crepes with piping hot maple syrup; sweet and juicy strawberries; and brewed English tea with cream. A tiny bud vase would hold one lily. The newspaper would be folded over once. Horowitz would be playing Bach's *Partita Number 4*, just for me. And I would be smiling.

Then again, perhaps I really prefer the buffet table filled with a variety of china serving dishes showing off the scrambled eggs with corned beef hash; the potatoes well done in the oven and smothered in onions; a freshly baked wheat bread; bananas in cream; and a thirst-quenching pitcher of sangria (with oranges and lemons, naturally). We'd be gathered around the television, watching the Miami Dolphins cream the Dallas Cowboys. The room would ring with the happy sounds of friends chattering and laughing and having a grand old time.

I love breakfast! Always have! It's the beginning of what always promises to be yet another great day. My way to give the day the start it deserves is to make sure that I fill my body with the best food, making each breakfast, whether it's simple or deliciously elaborate, the ultimate. It can be on a yacht—but it doesn't have to be, and rarely is. Mostly it is in my kitchen, cooked on my everyday, ordinary stove—a simple but delicious meal prepared in no time and eaten with relish and a smile. Sometimes, as often as possible, it is with friends. Relaxed, at ease, not dressed to the nines or prepared for a proper, formal meal, we exchange jokes and stories and events of the day or week while we heartily eat whatever splendid foods I have prepared.

I've been making breakfasts for over 20 years. Not just for myself— that I've been doing quite a bit longer, ever since my mother sent me off aboard ship to conquer the world. But for others, on my two-burner stove in my small restaurant, Scully's, in Beverly Hills, California. I have been making these breakfasts five days a week (and eating them at least as often, sometimes twice a day!). That's about 5,000 mornings of eggs and pancakes and hash and sausage and bread— and I'm not bored nor am I finished. I intend to keep on making breakfasts as long as I can still make them the ultimate, and as long as people keep on coming.

I didn't start out to be a cook. Actually, I'm not sure what I started out to be. But the fact is that I was born in 1933, in Liverpool, England. When I was 15 I decided to go away to sea—that was the thing to do in those days—romantic, adventurous boys always "went to sea." I got a job on a boat called *The Green Goddess*, an absolutely sensational boat—it cost $30,000 for a suite in those days, so you can imagine the luxury! I remember that the carpet covered my shoes, the silverware always seemed virginally unused, and the kitchen was open 24 hours a day.

I started as a bellhop, complete with a Philip Morris uniform. Soon they made me a commis waiter—that meant I got to help the real waiter. I loved it—I learned everything I could about serving food, and the rest of the time I sat in the sun on deck. I know I was enthusiastic, and I guess I was good, because after three trips they made me a waiter. They said it was because I was a good learner and a hard worker, but frankly, I always suspected it was because I grew out of my commis waiter's jacket. (I was huge even then!)

I did learn. I soon became my own expert about silver, service, and serving—and most important of all, what was good food, and how to serve it first class. And when I left this boat to work on some others—the *Queen Mary*, the *Queen Elizabeth*, and the *Ocean Monarch*—I took that knowledge and experience with me and kept on learning. And I loved what I did—I loved the adventure, of course, but I loved being around entertaining. I relished the fine service, the beauty and taste of good food, and the pleasure of seeing people having a wonderful time. I always got a kick out of serving a great meal and watching people enjoy the food and the atmosphere. (I still get a charge out of seeing people having fun at one of my tables!) I really never wanted to do anything else. I just wanted to create wonderful meals, and to have fun doing it.

Eventually I got tired of my sea legs, so in 1955 I went to live in Bermuda. I stayed there for three years as a room-service captain in a hotel, and that's where I began serving breakfasts to the guests in their rooms. Work began very early in the morning, and to my surprise, I found that I actually preferred that time of day—I enjoyed waking up with the morning air to prepare that first meal that I knew would start my guests off to a great day. What a perfect life!

And it was. After all, serving breakfasts for my guests turned out to be a six-hour day, which I considered enough for any man. And, let's be honest, that schedule gave me the afternoon in the sun, which I considered essential to my well-being. After a while I decided that I had learned what I could, and since Bermuda had begun to seem too small for me, I traveled around a bit and ended up in Los Angeles.

It didn't take me long to figure out that there were hotels and restaurants everywhere, and one of them was sure to be waiting for me to show them my talents. I got a job as a waiter at the famous Beverly Hills Hotel, working in the Lanai Room. The food was just okay, but the place was great, the service was nice, and the captains' uniforms were terrific. So I thought to myself, "Hey—this is a classy place. I could use some classy training. Let's give it a try." And thus I started my California career.

Then, one fateful day, the hotel management decided that I would have to work the dinner shift. What? No more breakfasts? No more serving morning creations to start off my guests' days? Serve dinner? Me? And no afternoons at the beach? Something was awry—this was not in my plans. So I quit. And no sooner had I left than I found out that the most famous restaurant in Los Angeles—Chasen's—was looking for a waiter. Now this sounded great. Here I could do it all—I was a waiter, I could cook, I could bartend—and here I would be able to practice all these skills in a restaurant that, in those days, represented the height of glamour. Chasen's had the name, the nostalgia, the stars—and great food. So I took the job.

I stayed sixteen years. I worked large parties—for Elizabeth Taylor, Henry Kissinger, Ronald Reagan, Gene Kelly, Nat King Cole—and small dinners for two. I served breakfasts in bed and breakfast for 700. (That was the CBS Annual Affiliates Meeting—can you imagine making scrambled eggs [or eggs, any style] and bacon for that many visitors, most of whom had already consumed their share of Bloody Marys by 10 o'clock in the morning!) I cooked for John F. Kennedy, for Sinatra, for Nixon and Humphrey and Burton.

They all came, and I cooked for them all. And many times they would call me to come to their homes to cook for them—and I did that, too—whether it was breakfast for Gregory Peck or for Hubert Humphrey at Eugene Klein's, or a brunch for Alfred Hitchcock when he was in the hospital, or late breakfast for Liz and Richard when they were encamped in their bungalow at the Beverly Hills Hotel. (Liz loved the Caesar salad at Chasen's, and even when she was staying at the Beverly Hills Hotel she would call and have me bring her Chasen's salad. One night Ben Silverstein, the owner of the hotel, caught me bringing the salad up to Liz. He asked me what was wrong with his Caesar salad, and I replied, quite simply, "It's like soup, Mr. Silverstein. It won't do for Elizabeth Taylor.")

The more I cooked, the more I learned. I found that I had the touch for inventing dishes that guests requested. I learned that I could take a dish and give it my own touch—and the customers loved it. (I'll never forget J. Edgar Hoover's delight at the taste of my enchiladas!) I began to experiment and found that I could bring my own touch to the beef Wellington, the soufflé, the seafood, and the eggs Benedict.

I loved it. I cared about the freshness of the food, I cared about the ingredients, I cared about the taste and how it all looked. And that made me different. I knew I didn't belong there, not forever. Even then I knew that I would have to open Scully's.

How do I honestly describe Scully's? Well, I guess I have to start by telling you that it is on the ground floor of a not-very-noticeable but well-known motel on the outskirts of Beverly Hills. It is a very small restaurant—I started with only 9 tables (I now have 13). There is no sign on the door, and the telephone number is unlisted. Some people think that's snobbish. I suppose this is a bit cocky, but it's also practical. Because Scully's *is* so small, and it can accommodate only about 30 people at one time, I don't advertise its existence either by ads or by having the name outside. People somehow know it's there. They first started coming ten years ago. They told their friends, who told theirs. And the same people keep coming back.

My guests know that at Scully's they'll be noticed, admired, respected, and ribbed. But they also know that they'll be comfortable, as if they were eating in a friend's home. They know that if they wish for privacy, that's what they'll get. If they want to gossip with the other guests, they'll have plenty of opportunity to exchange stories. And they know that the food will always be fresh, that it is always made just for them while they wait, that it will be delicious.

The front room at Scully's is also the only room at Scully's. It looks like the front parlor of an old English home, one you'd be happy to bring Mum to, if you like, or the president of NBC. On any given day you'll find a lot of happy faces, some anonymous, others well known. Besides my old friends Robert Becker, Michael Durand, and Brian Gurnee, there are James Garner and Jack Lemmon and Neil Diamond devouring the corned beef hash; there are Mohammad Ali and Dolly Parton and Dave Tebbet (of NBC fame) and Victoria Principal and Larry Hagman relishing the homemade sausage. So are Dudley Moore and Vin Scully. And Barbara Sinatra and R. J. Wagner and Shirley Temple. There's Deborah Raffin eating the broccoli with vinaigrette, and Richard Chamberlain and Sugar Ray Robinson ordering another round of enchiladas and eggs. They're all having fun. They're all loving their food.

The only other room at Scully's is the kitchen, and it is not much bigger than the kitchen in most homes. There is one refrigerator, two counters, and a two-burner stove.

You may find that hard to believe—running a restaurant where I cook at least 50 breakfasts and lunches every day on two burners. But it's easy. And that's why everything I make can be easily made at home. I have my so-called "Perfect Pantry" which holds everything I may need for that day's meals—the ones on the menu, and the ones my customers just have to have that day. I make some things ahead of time, just as you would. And I always have on hand the freshest ingredients, whether it's fresh eggs, smoked fish just flown in, meat, home-baked breads and marmalades, sour cream and fresh cream, and whatever fruits and vegetables are in season.

And that's it. I cook every dish when a guest orders it. The only other people in my kitchen are Joe Lopez, who has learned how to bake my bread and clean the mess I leave, and Melody, who serves the guests with me, and who otherwise runs my life my way.

And now I have a chance to share my food with you. Since most of you can't visit Scully's, I have brought my kitchen to you. In this book you will find the ultimate breakfasts that I have been serving at Scully's. They are, for the most part, easy to make. They are delicious, and beautiful when served—I want you to be able to enjoy breakfast as much as I do. Whether you'll eat alone, or entertain a motley group, do it with style; do it with humor; do it with great food!

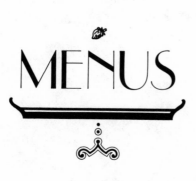

MENUS

BREAKFAST FOR TWO

MENU I

Popovers
Apple Omelet
Canadian Bacon
* Orange Marmalade
Coffee, Tea

MENU II

Baking Powder Biscuits
Sliced Oranges
Banana Dream Pancakes with
    Maple Syrup
Coffee, Tea

MENU III

Pumpernickel Bread
* Pickled Herring and Onions
Scully's French Toast
Baked Apples
Coffee, Tea

BREAKFAST FOR FOUR

MENU I

Fresh Papaya and
    Strawberries
Onion Soufflé
* Honey Cake
Coffee, Tea

MENU II

English Scones
Boysenberry Omelet
* Custard Wild Rice Pudding
Coffee, Tea

* These recipes can be prepared the day before.

MENU III
* Date-Nut Bread
  Spinach Ricotta Crepes
* Orange Marmalade
* Egg-and-Cheese Custard
* Chocolate Chip Cookies
  Coffee, Tea

BREAKFAST FOR EIGHT

MENU I

Corn Fritters
Curried Chopped Egg Salad
Fluffy Yogurt Pancakes
Sautéed Mushrooms on Toast
* Honey Cake
Fresh Fruit
Coffee, Tea

MENU II

* Banana Bread
* Tuna Salad
* Blintzes
* Noodle-Oyster and Clam Loaf
    with Creamed Eggs
* Doughnuts
  Coffee, Tea

MENU III
* Eggnog
  Buttermilk Biscuits
  Eggs in Potato Boats
* Homemade Sausage
  Chocolate Bread Pudding
  Coffee, Tea

BUFFET BREAKFAST FOR 12–16

MENU I

Berries in Devon Cream
Steak Tartar
Chile Relleno
Tacos
Green Salad with Honey-Dill
    Dressing
* Doughnuts
* Sorbets
  Coffee, Tea

MENU II

* Smoked Trout
  Cheese Potatoes
  Onions and Eggs
* Dill Bread
* Mashed Potato Doughnuts
* Tangerines in Kirsch
  Coffee, Tea

MENU III
Vichyssoise
Green Salad or Steamed Broccoli
*with * Basil Dressing*
* *Creamed Chipped Corned Beef*
Eggs Indian
* *Almond Tart*
* *Coffee Cake*
Coffee, Tea

BREAKFAST AT MIDNIGHT, FOR TWO

Welsh Rarebit
* *Strawberry Amour*
Cocoa with Kahlúa

THE FANTASY BREAKFAST, FOR TWO

Raspberries in Devon Cream with Kirsch
* *Scotch Eggs*
Coffee Soufflé
Coffee, Tea

THE REUNION BREAKFAST, FOR 6–8

* *Cranberry Muffins*
Potato Pancakes
* *White Beans and Tuna*
Bacon
Melody's Zabaglione
Coffee, Tea

OPEN-HOUSE BREAKFAST, FOR 12–20

Sangria
* *Cold Curry Soup*
Mexican Eggs
* *Corned Beef Hash*
* *Salmon Quiche*
Home-Fried Potatoes
* *Ultimate Chocolate Cake*
Coffee, Tea

LOVELY, LONELY BREAKFAST FOR ONE

* *Sweet Muffins*
  Apple Crepes with Bacon
  Bread and Butter Pudding
  Coffee, Tea

THE TENNIS BREAKFAST, FOR 4–6

* *Gazpacho with Tortillas*
* *Codfish Salad*
* *Chicken Pasta Salad*
  Cheese Toast
* *Carrot Cake*
  Fresh Fruit
* *Sorbets*
  Iced Tea

VALENTINE'S BREAKFAST FOR TWO

Champagne
Popovers
Heaven's Gate Omelet
Strawberries with Devon Cream
Café au Lait

THE ANNIVERSARY BREAKFAST, FOR ONE

Champagne
* *Orange Bread*
  Russian Eggs
  Chocolate Soufflé
  Calypso Coffee

THE ULTIMATE BREAKFAST FOR TWO

* *Irish Soda Bread*
  Eggs from Heaven
  Zabaglione
  Irish Coffee

FOOTBALL FEAST, FOR 8–10

Sangria
Fried Tortillas and Eggs
* *Salsa*
* *Fish Cakes*
Cheese Potatoes
* *Chocolate Chip Cookies*
* *Ice Cream*
Coffee, Tea

THE POT-LUCK BREAKFAST, FOR 4–6

* *Corn Muffins*
Kitchen Sink Omelet and Bacon
Home-Fried Potatoes
* *Baked Apples*
Coffee, Tea

BREAKFAST BY THE POOL, FOR 6–8

Cold Cucumber Soup
Stuffed Eggs with Crabmeat
Smoked Salmon and Bagels
Chocolate Bread Pudding
Iced Cinnamon Coffee
Iced Tea

RAINY SUNDAY IN BED BREAKFAST, FOR TWO

Smoked Sturgeon Sandwich
Sweet Crepes
Strawberries or Blueberries in Devon Cream
Coffee, Tea

THE "JUST BECAUSE" BREAKFAST, FOR 2–3

* *Chicken Liver Pâté*
Cheese Soufflé
Raspberries or Strawberries in Cream
Coffee, Tea

THE MORNING-AFTER BREAKFAST, FOR TWO

Strawberry Wine Daiquiris
* *Basic White Bread, Toasted*
* *Smoked Trout*
Chocolate Waffles
Coffee Brûlé

SPRINGTIME BREAKFAST, FOR 4–6

* *Sesame Bread*
Anchovy Salad
Everyday Extraordinary Waffles
Papaya and Berries
Iced Coffee

BIRTHDAY BREAKFAST BASH, FOR 8–10

Champagne
Beer-Batter Crepes
Eggs Diablo
Steak Tartar
* *Ultimate Chocolate Cake*
Coffee, Tea

NEW YEAR'S DAY FEAST, FOR 8–10

Long Tail
Raclette
Poached Eggs Gourmet
Chicken Livers
* *Cajun Crab Cakes*
Escargots with Mushrooms
* *Ice Cream*
Irish Coffee

MOTHER'S OR FATHER'S DAY BREAKFAST, FOR 4–6

* *Dill Bread*
* *Orange Marmalade*
Ricotta Pancakes
* *Ultimate Chocolate Cake*
Coffee, Tea

THE FAMILY SUNDAY BREAKFAST, FOR 4–6

* Mexican Muffins
  Eggs Ranchero
* Homemade Sausage
* Egg-and-Cheese Custard
  Fireplace Coffee

THE HOUSEWARMING BREAKFAST, FOR 10–12

Bloody Tequila Marys
* Whole-Wheat Bread
* Corn Muffins
  Kippers and Eggs
* Pork Stew Chile Verde
  French Toast Princess Di
* Chocolate Cream Pudding
  Coffee, Tea

THE HANGOVER BREAKFAST, FOR ONE

* Banana Bread
  Brie Cheese
  Eggs from Heaven
  Black Velvet

THE FAMILY CHRISTMAS BREAKFAST, FOR 4–6

* Eggnog
  Cold Mushroom Soup
* Chicken à la King
* Homemade Sausage
  Janet's Blue Cheese Omelet
* Ultimate Chocolate Cake
  Coffee, Tea

THE LOW-CAL, LOW-CHOLESTEROL BREAKFAST, FOR ONE

Oatmeal with Apple Juice
* Whole-Wheat Bread
  Fresh Papaya with Strawberries
  Black Coffee or Constant Comment Tea

RECIPES

FRUITS

BAKED APPLES

4 *large Granny Smith apples*
½ *cup raisins*
½ *cup apple juice*
2 *tablespoons butter or margarine, melted*
  Pinch of ground cinnamon
1 *teaspoon confectioner's sugar*

Preheat oven to 350°.

Core apples. (Make a nice, clean cut, removing all seeds.) Do not peel. Stuff with raisins. Place in a large baking dish (or, if you wish, individual baking dishes). Pour apple juice on the bottom. Brush each apple with melted butter and sprinkle with cinnamon and confectioner's sugar.

Bake at 350° for about 40 minutes. When brown, remove from oven and cool. Serve plain or with heavy cream.

Hint: If you want the apples to retain their green color, you can soak them before filling for 30 minutes in cold water to which you have added 1 teaspoon fresh lemon juice.

Another Hint: When storing apples, if you keep them from touching one another they will retain their smoothness.

Serves 4

MORNING GRAPEFRUIT

> 1 grapefruit
> 1/8 cup cognac
> 2 tablespoons brown sugar

Preheat oven to Broil or 350°.

Cut 1 inch off top of grapefruit. Pit and section. Pour cognac over fruit and top with brown sugar. Place under broiler for 5 to 10 minutes or until sugar is browned, or bake at 350° for 20 minutes. Serve warm.

Serves 1

SLICED ORANGES

> 2 large oranges, peeled, seeded, and sliced
> 2 tablespoons kirsch or Courvoisier (optional)
> Fresh mint leaves (optional)

Place the orange slices in a glass bowl. They are great served this simply—but for that extra touch, spoon 2 tablespoons of your favorite liqueur (kirsch, Courvoisier, or the like) over the top. Cover and marinate for 30 minutes.

Serve in a pretty glass bowl with fresh mint leaves as a garnish.

Serves 2

STRAWBERRIES IN CREAM

Any fresh berry in fresh cream is a breakfast treat. Whether you start or finish off your breakfast with them, you'll be in heaven.

> 2 cups hulled fresh strawberries (or any berry you love)
> 1/4 teaspoon vanilla
> 1 cup heavy or Devon Cream (see page 166)

My secret is to use only the freshest, ripest strawberries (blueberries, raspberries, blackberries, boysenberries), covered with the freshest cream. If using heavy cream, add vanilla before whipping. I recommend that you whip the cream until it is smooth but still runny, so that it looks more like crème fraîche. Neatly layer the hulled fresh berries into a pretty bowl and top with cream. Serve immediately.

Serves 4

Hint: If you like, you can also add liqueur to the cream before you whip it.

LIQUEURED TANGERINES OR PEACHES

This one is easy and delicious! It's fine to make it the night before; it will take little time and will leave you free to make breakfast in the morning without having to worry about a fruit or a dessert. Besides, it is so refreshing on either summer or winter mornings!

> *4 tangerines or peaches*
> *2 tablespoons confectioner's sugar*
> *2 tablespoons Courvoisier*

Peel the tangerines and separate into segments. Remove membrane. If using peaches, halve and remove pits. Arrange fruit in individual serving dishes; sprinkle with confectioner's sugar and liqueur. Refrigerate, covered, for at least 2 hours or overnight.

Serves 4

BREADS
AND
MUFFINS

BASIC WHITE BREAD

6 *packets dry yeast*
5 *cups warm water*
½ *cup sugar*
½ *cup butter, melted*
5 *pounds all-purpose flour*
1 *teaspoon salt (optional—I really don't use salt in my bread recipes, but if you must have it, don't use more than this)*
6 *mini loaf pans (5¾ × 3 × 2⅛ inches)*

Place yeast in a small glass bowl. Stir in 1 cup warm water and the sugar. (Adding the sugar at this point activates the yeast more quickly.)

When the yeast foams, in about 15 minutes, put it into the food processor. Add the melted butter, flour, salt if used, and remaining water, mixing with the steel blade as you add (you will need to make it in two batches). When well blended, mix for another 5 minutes or until the dough is shiny and elastic.

Remove the dough and place it in a large, greased bowl. Cover with a towel and set in a warm place until it has risen to double its size, about 1½ hours.

Grease and flour the mini loaf pans. Place the bread dough on a floured board, sprinkle with a little flour, and cut into six separate pieces. Knead each piece for about 5 minutes, shape into rolls, and place one in each pan. Set the pans in a warm place, cover, and let dough rise to double its size.

Preheat oven to 350°.

When the dough has risen 1 inch above the top of each pan, gently place on the top shelf of the preheated oven and bake for 55 minutes or until golden brown. Remove loaves from pan and cool on wire racks.

Makes 6 small loaves

Hint: Brush the warm bread with butter for a crisper crust.

Variation: For added flavor, add ½ cup grated Parmesan cheese to the flour.

SESAME BREAD

 3 *cups sifted all-purpose flour*
 1 *teaspoon salt*
3½ *teaspoons baking powder*
 ½ *cup toasted sesame seeds*
 1 *cup sugar*
 ¼ *cup sweet butter or margarine, melted*
 2 *eggs*
 1 *teaspoon freshly grated lemon rind*
1⅓ *cups milk*
 1 *tablespoon untoasted sesame seeds*

Preheat oven to 350°.

Sift together the flour, salt, and baking powder. Add the toasted sesame seeds. Beat the sugar, butter, and eggs together. Add the lemon rind and milk. Pour into the flour mixture and gently blend.

Grease and flour a 7½ × 3½ × 2-inch loaf pan and pour in batter. Sprinkle top with untoasted sesame seeds. Bake in preheated oven for 1 hour and 15 minutes or until golden. Remove from pan and cool on wire rack.

Makes 1 loaf

WHOLE-WHEAT BREAD

6 packets dry yeast
5 cups warm water
½ cup sugar
½ cup butter, melted
5 pounds whole-wheat flour
1 teaspoon salt (optional)
5 to 6 mini loaf pans (5¾ × 3 × 2⅛ inches)

Place yeast in a small glass bowl. Stir in 1 cup warm water and the sugar. (Adding the sugar at this point activates the yeast more quickly.)

When the yeast foams, in about 15 minutes, put it into the food processor. Add melted butter, flour, salt if used, and remaining water, mixing with the steel blade as you add. (You will need to make it in two batches.) When blended, mix for another 5 minutes or until the dough is shiny and elastic.

Remove the dough and place it in a large, greased bowl. Cover with a towel and set in a warm place until it has risen to double its size, about 1½ to 2 hours.

Grease and flour the mini loaf pans. Place the bread dough on a floured board, sprinkle with a little flour, and cut into six separate pieces. Knead each piece for about 5 minutes, shape into rolls, and place one in each pan. Set the pans in a warm place, cover, and let dough rise to double its size.

Preheat oven to 350°.

When dough has risen 1 inch above the top of each pan, gently place on the top shelf of the preheated oven and bake for 55 minutes or until golden brown. Remove from pans and cool on wire racks. These loaves are small enough so that you can give one to each guest.

Makes 6 small loaves

Hint: Brush the warm bread with butter for a nice crust.

Another Hint: To check if the bread is cooked, tap top gently with a knife. If it sounds hollow, it is done.

BANANA BREAD

½ *cup sweet butter or margarine*
¾ *cup brown sugar*
1 *egg*
1 *cup unsifted whole-wheat flour*
½ *cup unsifted all-purpose flour*
1 *teaspoon baking soda*
½ *teaspoon salt (optional)*
¼ *teaspoon ground cinnamon*
2 or 3 *ripe bananas, mashed*
¼ *cup buttermilk or nonfat plain yogurt*
1 *cup chopped walnuts (optional)*

Preheat oven to 350°.

In the food processor, using the steel blade, blend the butter or margarine with the sugar until the mixture turns a light brown. Beat in the egg. Remove from processor bowl and set aside.

In a large mixing bowl, sift together the flours, baking soda, salt, and cinnamon.

Using the food processor with metal blade, blend together the bananas and buttermilk.

Alternately add banana and butter mixtures to the flour, mixing thoroughly after each addition. When well mixed, fold in walnuts.

Grease and flour a 9 × 5-inch loaf pan. Pour the mixture into the prepared pan and bake in preheated oven for 1 hour or until a knife inserted into the middle of the bread comes out clean.

Remove from oven and let stand for 15 minutes. Remove from pan and refrigerate for at least 1 hour before using. When cool, serve immediately. To store, wrap tightly in plastic wrap and refrigerate.

Makes 1 loaf

Hint: If you try to cut this bread when you take it out of the oven, it will crumble. It is particularly good when it is cold and can be used just as you would any white bread.

IRISH SODA BREAD

You can make this bread first thing in the morning. Just watch your guests' faces as they walk into your home and smell the fresh bread baking! (You can also successfully double this recipe.)

2 cups sifted all-purpose flour
¾ teaspoon baking soda
½ teaspoon salt
1 tablespoon sugar
6 tablespoons butter or margarine
½ cup raisins
1 tablespoon caraway seeds
½ cup buttermilk
⅓ cup Irish whiskey
2 tablespoons milk

Preheat oven to 375°.

Sift together the flour, baking soda, salt, and sugar. Cut butter into the flour until coarse and crumbly. Stir in raisins and caraway seeds. Slowly add buttermilk and whiskey. Knead into the shape of a round loaf.

Place loaf on a greased baking sheet. Make a cut in the top of the dough with a knife. Brush with milk. Bake in preheated oven for 45 minutes or until golden brown. Remove from heat and cool on wire rack.

Makes 1 loaf

Hint: This bread, wrapped in a towel in an airtight tin, will keep, refrigerated, for a week. It makes great toast every morning.

DILL BREAD

I love dill! It is so versatile, plus it is easy to grow (even on your kitchen counter). You have probably used it in soups, in salads, or on eggs—and here it is in a wonderful bread!

¼ cup warm water
1 packet dry yeast
2 tablespoons chopped fresh dill
1 cup cottage cheese
1 tablespoon butter or margarine
2 tablespoons sugar
1 egg
1 teaspoon baking soda
½ teaspoon salt
2½ cups sifted all-purpose flour

Pour warm water into a small bowl. Add yeast and mix until dissolved. Add the dill, cheese, butter, sugar, egg, baking soda, and salt. Mix well. (You can do it in the food processor, if you like.)

Gradually add the flour, stirring constantly. Continue beating until a stiff dough is formed. Place the dough in a greased bowl and cover with a towel. Allow the dough to rise to double its size, about 1 hour.

Preheat oven to 350°.

Grease and flour a 2-quart (8 × 11½ inches) glass baking dish. Shape the dough into a loaf and place in the dish. Cover with a towel and set in a warm place. Let rise for 30 minutes. Put in preheated oven and bake for about 45 minutes or until golden. Remove from heat and let cool on wire rack.

Makes 1 loaf

Hint: You must let freshly baked bread cool before you try to slice it or it will break apart. To further ensure that the slices don't crumble, heat a serrated knife and then cut.

DATE-NUT BREAD WITH ORANGE ICING

1½ *cups boiling water*
 1 *10-ounce package pitted dates, quartered*
1¼ *cups sugar*
 1 *tablespoon sweet butter or margarine*
2¾ *cups sifted all-purpose flour*
 1 *teaspoon baking soda*
 ½ *teaspoon salt*
 1 *egg, beaten*
 1 *teaspoon vanilla*
 ¾ *cup chopped nuts*

Preheat oven to 350°.

Pour boiling water over dates, sugar, and butter or margarine in a medium saucepan. Cook over low heat for 5 minutes, stirring constantly. Remove from heat and let cool. By hand, mix in the flour, baking soda, and salt. Stir in the egg, vanilla, and nuts and blend well.

Grease and flour a medium (7½ × 3½ × 2-inch) loaf pan. Fill with batter and bake in preheated oven for about 1 hour or until brown. Remove from oven and cool on wire rack. When cool, spread with orange icing, if desired.

Makes 1 loaf

Orange Icing

2 *teaspoons freshly grated orange rind*
1 *cup confectioner's sugar*
2 *tablespoons sweet butter*
2 *tablespoons fresh orange juice*
1 *tablespoon milk*
½ *teaspoon vanilla*

In a small bowl, beat the rind, sugar, and butter. Add the orange juice, milk, and vanilla and continue mixing until well blended. Spread on the cooled date bread. Slice and serve.

Hint: Serve with strong brewed English tea and cream. This is also a great lunchbox bread—it stays fresh and gets better with age. Uniced, it is good plain or as a sandwich with a cream cheese and jam filling.

ORANGE BREAD

The taste of orange in this bread is a wonderful surprise.

> 3 *cups sifted all-purpose flour*
> 3 *teaspoons baking powder*
> 1 *tablespoon freshly grated orange rind*
> 1 *cup sugar*
> 1 *teaspoon vanilla*
> 1 *egg*
> ⅓ *cup fresh orange juice*
> 1⅓ *cups milk*
> 2 *tablespoons butter or margarine, melted*
> ½ *cup chopped walnuts (optional)*

Preheat oven to 350°.

In a large mixing bowl, sift 3 cups of flour, then measure it again. You need 3 cups of *well-sifted* flour. Add the baking powder and sift again. Stir in the orange rind and sugar. Set aside.

In another bowl, or in the food processor, blend the vanilla, egg, juice, milk, and butter or margarine. When blended, pour into a mixing bowl and add nuts. Stir in flour mixture until just blended. (Do not use the food processor—mix by hand, as the ingredients should be lightly blended.)

Grease and flour two 8 × 4-inch loaf pans. Pour half the batter into each pan. Bake in preheated oven for about 45 minutes or until golden brown. Set aside for 20 minutes to cool. Remove from pans and refrigerate for ½ hour before serving.

Makes 2 loaves

Hint: This is a great bread to make the day before needed. Refrigerate, then heat in the toaster oven for a few minutes just as your guests arrive. It is also a great treat with eggs, salad, or alone with my Homemade Orange Marmalade (see page 174).

BAKING POWDER BISCUITS

2 cups all-purpose flour
1 tablespoon baking powder
½ teaspoon salt
⅓ cup safflower oil or sweet butter
¾ cup milk

Preheat oven to 450°.

Mix together the flour, baking powder, and salt. Stir in the oil and mix with a fork until the mixture resembles coarse crumbs. With a wooden spoon, make a well in the middle. Pour in the milk. Stir until dough just clings together. Turn out of bowl and knead gently on a lightly floured surface.

Using a rolling pin, roll the dough to ½-inch thickness. Cut with a 2½-inch biscuit cutter.

Grease a baking sheet and place biscuits on it, at least 1 inch apart. Bake in preheated oven for about 12 minutes or until golden brown. Remove from oven and serve immediately.

Makes 12 biscuits

> **Buttermilk Biscuits.** *If you want to make buttermilk biscuits, substitute buttermilk for milk and add ¼ teaspoon baking soda to the flour. If this is a last-minute decision and you don't have any buttermilk, blend nonfat plain yogurt in the food processor with the steel blade. It will have the consistency of buttermilk and may be used as a substitute.*
>
> *Serve with strawberries or with Devon Cream (see page 166), sour cream, or melted butter and jam. For a different treat, make Easy Gravy (see page 166), pour it over the biscuits, and serve with mashed potatoes and poached eggs.*

Hint: If you dip the biscuit cutter in flour between cuttings, the biscuit edges will be neater.

Another Hint: Store biscuits in an airtight container with a tissue inside to absorb the moisture. Don't put them in a container with cake, as it will make the biscuits soft.

ENGLISH SCONES

2 *cups all-purpose flour*
1/4 *teaspoon salt*
1/2 *cup sugar*
3 *teaspoons baking powder*
1/2 *cup butter*
1 *cup raisins*
2 *eggs, beaten*
1/3 *cup milk*
1 *tablespoon flour, for dusting*

Preheat oven to 400°.

In a medium bowl, sift together the flour, salt, sugar, and baking powder. Cut the butter into small pieces and, using a knife, cut into the flour until crumbly. Add the raisins.

Beat the eggs into the mixture. Add the milk and stir to blend.

Grease and dust a baking sheet. On a floured surface, pat the dough out to a circle about ¾ inch thick. Cut the dough into wedges and place on the sheet. Bake in preheated oven for about 20 minutes or until lightly browned.

The scones should indent slightly on top when done. Remove from heat and place on wire racks to cool. Serve with Devon Cream (see page 166), sour cream, fresh strawberries, and/or any jam.

Makes 12 scones

These are wonderful for breakfast and don't take long to make. Serve with English tea (no lemon, just cream) or cappuccino. Fabulous!

CORN FRITTERS

1 *8-ounce can whole-kernel corn, drained*
¾ *cup sautéed chopped onions*
1 *egg, beaten*
1 *tablespoon chopped fresh parsley*
2 *teaspoons sugar*
½ *teaspoon salt*
½ *teaspoon Trassi Udang* (optional)*
1 *teaspoon Laos* (optional)*
2 *scallions, chopped*
½ *cup chopped cooked shrimp*
¼ *cup milk*
1 *teaspoon powdered coriander*
2 *cloves garlic, mashed*
¼ *cup sifted all-purpose flour*
2 *cups safflower oil, for frying*
2 *tablespoons chopped fresh cilantro, for garnish*
1 *tablespoon chopped fresh mint, for garnish*

Place all the ingredients except oil and garnish in a medium-size mixing bowl and blend thoroughly. In a deep iron pot, heat the oil until it is very hot. Drop the batter by the teaspoonful into the pot. Deep-fry the fritters until golden brown on both sides. When done, remove from oil. Drain on paper towels and serve immediately sprinkled with chopped fresh cilantro and mint.

Makes 8 fritters

* These Eastern spices are found in most Oriental markets.

POPOVERS

Most people think that popovers are *so* hard to make. Not true! This is such a simple recipe, you can have popovers every morning!

2 *eggs*
1 *cup milk*
1 *cup sifted all-purpose flour*
½ *teaspoon salt (optional)*

Beat the eggs lightly. Add the milk, sifted flour, and salt. Mix gently with a fork, leaving lumps. They are supposed to be there!

Grease a 6-cup muffin pan or, better yet, a popover pan (made of heavy cast iron and, if you love popovers, a wise investment). Fill each cup about three-quarters full and place in a cold oven. Turn the oven to 450° and bake for 20 minutes or until the popovers rise and blossom.

Serve immediately, before they fall, with butter and/or jam.

Makes 6 popovers

Hint: If your popover pan has eight cups, make sure you fill the two empty cups three-quarters full of water.

INDIAN MUFFINS

2 *cups all-purpose flour*
3 *tablespoons sugar*
1 *teaspoon baking powder*
½ *teaspoon ground nutmeg*
¼ *teaspoon ground cloves*
¼ *teaspoon ground cinnamon*
2 *eggs*
1 *cup milk*
¼ *cup butter*
½ *cup raisins*
¼ *cup chopped nuts*

Preheat oven to 375°.

Grease and flour a 12-cup muffin pan. Mix together the flour, sugar, baking powder, nutmeg, cloves, and cinnamon.

Beat together the eggs and milk. Add the butter. Fold into the flour mixture until well blended. Add the raisins and nuts. Fill each muffin cup three-quarters full.

Bake for about 20 minutes or until light brown. (These muffins can be frozen and reheated.)

Makes 12 muffins

BLUEBERRY BRAN MUFFINS

3 *cups bran cereal*
1 *cup boiling water*
½ *cup safflower oil*
2 *eggs*
2½ *cups all-purpose flour*
1½ *cups sugar*
1 *tablespoon baking soda*
2 *cups buttermilk*
1 *cup fresh or frozen blueberries*

Preheat oven to 400°.

Grease and flour a 12-cup muffin pan. Set aside. Mix the cereal and boiling water until well soaked. Add the oil and eggs and blend thoroughly. Add the flour, sugar, baking soda, and buttermilk. When well mixed, add the blueberries and carefully stir with a wooden spoon so as not to break the berries.

Fill muffin cups three-quarters full. Bake for 20 minutes or until golden brown. Serve warm.

Makes 12 muffins

CRANBERRY MUFFINS

2 *cups sifted all-purpose flour*
1 *tablespoon baking powder*
1 *tablespoon sugar*
1 *egg, beaten*
1 *cup milk*
1 *cup whole, fresh cranberries*
¼ *cup butter or margarine, melted*

Preheat oven to 400°.

Sift together the flour, baking powder, and sugar. Add the beaten egg, milk, and cranberries. Mix gently with a wooden spoon until well blended. Do not mix in the food processor as the cranberries will break. Stir in the melted butter or margarine.

Grease and flour a 12-cup muffin pan. Fill each muffin cup two-thirds full and bake for about 20 minutes or until light brown. Remove from heat and serve warm.

Makes 12 muffins

Hint: Soak cranberries overnight in 1 ounce bourbon.

CORN MUFFINS

There's nothing like a corn muffin fresh from the oven. I have come to love that homey smell early in the morning.

> 2 *cups sifted all-purpose flour*
> 2 *tablespoons sugar*
> 1 *tablespoon baking powder*
> 1 *cup yellow cornmeal*
>   *Pinch of salt*
> 1 *cup milk*
> 1 *egg, beaten*
> 4 *tablespoons sweet butter or margarine, melted*

Preheat oven to 375°.

Combine the flour, sugar, baking powder, cornmeal, and salt.

Blend the milk, egg, and melted butter or margarine. Pour into the flour mixture and stir gently, leaving batter slightly lumpy.

Grease and flour a 12-cup muffin tin and fill each cup two-thirds full. Bake for about 20 minutes or until brown. Remove from heat and serve immediately with butter and/or jam.

Makes 12 muffins

BLUE CHEESE MUFFINS

> 2 *cups all-purpose flour*
> 3 *tablespoons sugar*
> ¼ *teaspoon salt*
> 1 *tablespoon baking powder*
> 1 *cup crumbled blue cheese*
> 1 *egg, beaten*
> 1 *cup milk*
> ¼ *cup safflower oil*

Preheat oven to 400°.

Grease an 8-cup muffin pan. Set aside. Blend the flour, sugar, salt, baking powder, and cheese. Mix together the egg, milk, and oil and stir into the dry mixture. Blend together until moist.

Fill muffin cups three-quarters full. Bake for 20 to 25 minutes or until golden brown. Serve warm.

Makes 8 muffins

BREAKFAST MUFFINS

> 2 *cups all-purpose flour*
> 3 *tablespoons sugar*
> 1 *tablespoon baking powder*
> 1 *egg, beaten*
> 1 *cup milk*
> ¼ *cup safflower oil*
> ½ *cup cooked and chopped bacon*

Preheat oven to 400°.

Grease and flour a 12-cup muffin pan. Set aside. Combine the flour, sugar, and baking powder. Add the egg, milk, and oil and beat until the batter is smooth. Add the bacon and stir to blend.

Fill the muffin cups three-quarters full. Bake for 20 minutes or until golden brown. Serve warm.

Makes 12 muffins

MEXICAN MUFFINS

    2 cups all-purpose flour
  2½ tablespoons sugar
    1 tablespoon baking powder
   ⅛ teaspoon chili powder
       Pinch of ground cumin
   ½ teaspoon salt
    1 egg, beaten
    1 8-ounce can creamed-style corn
   ⅓ cup milk
    3 tablespoons safflower oil
    2 tablespoons chopped fresh (or canned, if you prefer)
       green chili peppers
    2 tablespoons chopped pimento

Preheat oven to 400°.

In a mixing bowl, stir together the flour, sugar, baking powder, chili powder, cumin, and salt. Combine remaining ingredients and stir into the dry ingredients until just moistened.

Grease and flour a 12-cup muffin pan and fill each cup two-thirds full. Bake in preheated oven for 20 to 25 minutes or until golden. Remove from oven and serve immediately.

Makes 12 muffins

Hint: These muffins can be wrapped individually and frozen. Reheat them in the oven or toaster oven for 5 minutes. They will taste as if you had just made them.

Another Hint: Serve with fresh Cilantro Butter.

Cilantro Butter

In the food proccessor, using the steel blade, blend 1 tablespoon chopped fresh cilantro (remove the stems) with ½ cup butter. Refrigerate, covered, overnight.

SWEET MUFFINS

¼ cup sugar
1 teaspoon salt
¼ cup sweet butter, softened
1 packet dry yeast
¾ cup milk
1 egg
2 cups all-purpose flour
1 teaspoon ground nutmeg
½ teaspoon confectioner's sugar
½ teaspoon ground cinnamon (optional)

Preheat oven to 400°.

In the food processor, using the steel blade, mix together the sugar, salt, butter, yeast, milk, and egg until well blended. Add the flour and nutmeg and mix for about 1 minute. Scrape into a greased glass bowl. Cover with a towel and set aside in a warm place for an hour or until dough is nearly doubled in size.

Put dough in food-processor bowl and beat for 1 minute. Grease and flour an 8-cup muffin tin and fill each cup three-quarters full. Bake for 15 minutes or until light brown. Remove from heat and sprinkle muffins with confectioner's sugar or cinnamon. Serve warm.

Makes 8 muffins

Hint: Serve with pure maple syrup.

DOUGHNUTS

It's no trick to run down to the corner and buy 35 different varieties of doughnuts. The trick is to make them yourself—and the "trick" is so easy, you'll wonder why you ever bought prepared doughnuts.

>   ½ *cup granulated sugar*
>   1 *tablespoon melted butter*
>   2 *eggs*
>   1 *teaspoon vanilla*
>   ½ *cup milk*
>   2½ *cups all-purpose flour*
>   2½ *teaspoons baking powder*
>   ¼ *teaspoon salt*
>   ½ *teaspoon ground nutmeg*
>   *Safflower oil, for deep frying*
>   *Confectioner's sugar, cinnamon sugar,*
>   *chocolate glaze, or any coating you*
>   *prefer*

In the food processor, using the steel blade, mix together sugar, butter, and eggs. Add vanilla and milk and continue mixing.

In a separate bowl, sift together the flour, baking powder, salt, and nutmeg. Add to the sugar mixture and blend to make a soft dough.

Dust a cutting board with flour and roll out the dough to ½ inch thick. Using a doughnut cutter, cut out the dough.

Pour safflower oil into a deep pot to a depth of 4 inches. Heat until very hot. Drop the doughnuts into the oil one at a time. When golden brown, remove and drain on paper towels.

Dust, while warm, with confectioner's sugar, regular sugar, cinnamon sugar, or nutmeg, or cool slightly and glaze with chocolate or vanilla frosting.

Makes approximately 24 doughnuts

MASHED POTATO DOUGHNUTS

Chances are you won't find these at the corner store, so you have no choice—you'll have to make them!

> 2 *eggs*
> 4 *tablespoons melted butter*
> 1 *cup sugar*
> 1 *cup Mashed Potatoes (see page 110)*
> 1 *cup buttermilk*
> 4 *cups all-purpose flour*
> 3 *teaspoons baking powder*
> 1 *teaspoon salt*
> ½ *teaspoon baking soda*
> ½ *teaspoon ground nutmeg*
> 1 *cup safflower oil, for frying*
> 1 *pint nonfat plain yogurt (optional)*

In the food processor, using the steel blade, beat the eggs and the butter. While the processor is running, add the sugar, mashed potatoes, and buttermilk.

In a small bowl, sift together the flour, baking powder, salt, baking soda, and nutmeg. Add to the mashed-potato mixture and mix well.

Dust a cutting board with flour and roll out the dough to ½ inch thick.

In a heavy pan, heat the oil until it is very hot.

Using a doughnut cutter, cut out the dough. Drop the doughnuts one at a time into the oil and fry until golden brown. Remove and drain on paper towels. Serve warm. If you like, top with yogurt.

That's it!

Makes approximately 24 doughnuts

EASY LAST-MINUTE COFFEE CAKE

2 cups all-purpose flour
1 cup sugar
4 tablespoons cocoa
2 teaspoons baking soda
1 cup cold coffee
1 cup Mayonnaise (see page 173)
1 teaspoon vanilla

Preheat oven to 350°.

Mix all the dry ingredients together. Blend in the coffee, mayonnaise, and vanilla.

Grease and flour an 8-inch round cake pan. Pour in the batter and bake in preheated oven for 45 minutes. Test to see if it's done by inserting a knife in the middle. If it comes out clean, the cake is done. Remove from oven and cool on wire rack.

Slice and serve. It is delicious plain, spread with jam, or smothered in chocolate or coffee ice cream.

Makes 1 8-inch coffee cake

Hint: This is also great served with assorted jellies, sour cream or Devon Cream (see page 166), or sliced fresh fruit.

EGGS

General Egg Hints

1. Keep eggs refrigerated in their original container so they will stay fresh longer. Always buy the freshest, best quality eggs (check the date on the container) and buy fewer more often. There really is a difference between a fresh egg and one that has been on the market shelf for four days and in your refrigerator for a week. Once you have tasted a farm-fresh egg, you'll find it hard to eat any other kind.

2. If the egg is cracked when you take it out of the refrigerator, throw it out. It will have lost its freshness and also picked up the odors of other foods stored in the refrigerator.

3. If, as you should, you store both fresh and hard-boiled eggs but you've forgotten which is which, here's an easy trick my mother taught me: Spin the egg on a flat surface. The hard-boiled egg will spin beautifully; the fresh one will simply plop.

4. You can store egg yolks refrigerated for up to four days, covered with a little bit of water. Pour off the water before you use the yolks. Freeze egg whites in little plastic bags or in ice-cube trays. (I prefer the trays.) When frozen, I put the "egg cubes" into a plastic freezer bag for use when needed. Two tablespoons of defrosted egg whites are equal to one fresh egg white.

5. Generally allow three eggs per person—if someone joins you at the last minute, simply throw in an extra couple of eggs.

6. *Always* cook eggs over a low flame, slowly and gently.

7. Keeping eggs warm is easier than you think. Many of my egg dishes do not have to be made at the last minute. They can be made an hour ahead of time and kept warm in the following ways:

○ *Place the eggs on a platter, cover with aluminum foil, and put on an electric warming tray. They will stay warm for at least 30 minutes.*
○ *Keep the eggs covered in a chafing dish.*
○ *Serve the eggs on plates that have been warmed in the oven or dishwasher.*

8. When hard-boiling eggs, add 1 teaspoon salt to the water. This will make it easier to remove the shells. Put the eggs into cold water immediately after removing from the pot. This stops the cooking action and helps the shells slide off easily.

9. For light scrambled eggs, mix with a wooden spoon and keep stirring while cooking.

10. To check the freshness of an egg before poaching it, hold it up to the light—it should be transparent. Another way of checking is to put the egg in a bowl of salt water. If the egg goes to the bottom, it is fresh. If it stays in the middle of the water, it is two or three days old. If it floats, it's about five days old.

11. When you poach eggs, add a few drops of fresh lemon juice to the water to keep them from separating.

12. Cold eggs don't make good omelets. If you are planning to make omelets, take the eggs out of the refrigerator as soon as you get up. The reason most omelets aren't nice and fluffy is because the eggs are cooked directly from the refrigerator.

13. When making more than one omelet, it's a good idea to have three pans going so you can always have a hot one ready for flipping.

OMELETS

THE PLAIN, UNADULTERATED OMELET

Almost everyone makes omelets in one pan, flipping them over. I make them using two omelet pans. My omelets are chock-full of tasty fillings and if you tried to flip them, all the filling would slide out onto the stove or the floor and you'd be very upset. Even I, who have been making omelets for over 30 years, would lose the filling if I cooked in one pan. So, I still use two pans. I cook the omelet in one pan, and then merely flip it gently into the second pan onto its other side to cook the inside and the top. Haven't lost a filling in years!

First Method:

>*4 eggs, at room temperature or 3 eggs may be used*
>*2 tablespoons sweet butter or margarine*

Simple, and great. In a small bowl, with a fork or whisk, beat the eggs until well blended. In a small skillet, over low heat, melt 1 tablespoon of butter. Add the eggs and let a crust form on the bottom. While they are cooking, melt the other tablespoon of butter in another small skillet. When the omelet has formed a bottom crust, turn it over into the other skillet to finish cooking. When done, fold onto a plate and serve immediately.

You can garnish a plain omelet with a dab of sour cream, a teaspoon of caviar, chopped parsley, chopped tomatoes, a dab of fresh jam, or any other topping you like.

Serves 1 to 2

Second Method:

> 4 *egg yolks, at room temperature*
> ¼ *cup milk (optional)*
> 6 *egg whites*
> 2 *tablespoons sweet butter or margarine*

In the food processor, using the steel blade (or in a blender), beat the egg yolks and milk together until well blended. Let stand. Beat the egg whites until stiff. Gently fold whites into the egg-yolk mixture.

In a 6-inch skillet, over low heat, heat 1 tablespoon butter or margarine until hot. Do *not* let it brown. Pour the egg mixture into the pan and cook over low heat until the bottom is crusty. If there is a lot of moist egg left in the center, push the sides in with a wooden spoon to let the liquid run to the bottom of the pan.

As this is cooking, melt the other tablespoon of butter in the second skillet. When the omelet has formed a bottom crust, flip it over into the second pan to finish cooking. When crusty, remove from heat and fold onto a warm plate to serve.

This is a very fluffy omelet that will fall if not served immediately.

Serves 2

Both these omelets are very simple to make, so don't be afraid to do them for four to six guests. They take no time and you can turn them out easily. Ask your guests to help; they may love flipping omelets.

OMELET FILLINGS

Make the omelet according to recipe on page 46. To add a filling, place the filling on top of the omelet while the bottom crust is cooking. Don't be stingy—put plenty of filling on each one. When the bottom is crusty, flip the omelet over carefully into the second pan to cook the other side. This method will enclose the filling so it won't slip out of the omelet.

Fillings:

You may add salt and pepper to taste to any filling.

- *Mashed anchovies with grated Parmesan cheese (topping)*
- *Hearts of artichoke with grated Parmesan cheese (topping)*
- *Seafood—cooked shrimp, clams, and cheddar cheese; shredded smoked whitefish or salmon topped with cream cheese*
- *Sautéed or fresh mushrooms*
- *Diced potatoes, chopped chives, and chopped peeled apples*
- *Sautéed onions (cook slowly in butter to glaze)*
- *Oysters*
- *Diced potatoes and chopped parsley*
- *Chopped fresh apricots or chopped fresh figs, a touch of brandy, topped with sour cream and confectioner's sugar*
- *Crumbled cooked bacon*
- *Shredded cooked chicken and diced cooked tongue*
- *Chopped cooked chicken livers and onions or shallots*
- *Cooked whole fresh cranberries, topped with sour cream, a dash of bourbon, and a slice of orange*
- *2 tablespoons jam, jelly, or marmalade*
- *Sautéed chopped lamb kidneys*
- *Any steamed chopped vegetables*
- *Cooked rice pilaf*
- *Chopped tomatoes, cheddar cheese, and fresh basil*
- *Chopped cooked corned beef*
- *Chinese-style water chestnuts, minced onion, bean sprouts, diced cooked ham or bacon, chopped fresh cilantro, and Chinese seasonings*

○ *Sliced smoked mackerel*
○ *½ cup leftover pasta*
○ *Chopped mushrooms, dash of soy sauce, cooked ham, topped with shredded cheddar or Monterey Jack cheese*

APPLE OMELET

3 *tablespoons butter or margarine*
1 *green apple, cored and sliced*
1 *teaspoon raisins*
1 *teaspoon slivered almonds*
¼ *teaspoon brown sugar*
½ *teaspoon vanilla*
1 *tablespoon fresh lemon or lime juice*
4 *eggs*
1 *teaspoon confectioner's sugar*
1 *teaspoon sour cream for garnish (optional)*

In a small skillet, over medium heat, melt 1 tablespoon butter or margarine. Add the apple, raisins, and almonds. Sauté until the apple begins to soften. Stir in the brown sugar, vanilla, and lemon or lime juice. In a few minutes, a syrup will form and the apples will soften and brown. When brown, turn off the heat and set aside.

In another skillet, over medium heat, melt 2 tablespoons butter or margarine and make a 4-egg omelet (see page 46). Place the apple mixture in the middle of the omelet and cook until the bottom of the omelet is crusty. Turn the omelet into the skillet in which you pre-pared the apples and cook until done.

Remove to a warm platter, sprinkle with confectioner's sugar, and top with sour cream, if you wish.

Serves 1

Hint: You don't have to peel the apple, as the most nutritious part is the skin. But if you don't like the skin, peel it! Before slicing, you may also want to dip the apple slices in the lemon juice before you add the juice to the pan. This will keep the slices from turning brown before you cook them.

BELGIAN ENDIVE OMELET

2 *tablespoons butter or margarine*
1 *medium Belgian endive, shredded*
¼ *cup blanched almonds*
4 *eggs*
¼ *cup grated Swiss cheese*
¼ *cup grated mozzarella cheese*

In a large skillet, over medium heat, melt 1 tablespoon butter or margarine. Sauté the shredded endive and blanched almonds until the endive is soft (do not brown).

Beat the eggs. Melt the other tablespoon of butter or margarine in another skillet and make an omelet (see page 46). When bottom is crusty, put the endive and almonds in the center of the omelet. Sprinkle with the cheeses, reserving some cheese to sprinkle on top. Fold and place under the broiler for a minute to melt the cheese.

Serves 1

Hint: When you use endive, remove any dark outer leaves. I know endive is expensive, but the darker leaves taste bitter. Just use the pale inside leaves.

BOYSENBERRY OMELET

5 *egg yolks*
3 *tablespoons water*
8 *egg whites*
1 *tablespoon butter or margarine*
4 *tablespoons boysenberry jam (or other berry jam)*
1 *tablespoon confectioner's sugar (optional)*
2 *cups fresh boysenberries (or any other fresh berry; optional)*

In a small glass bowl, beat egg yolks with the water. Set aside.

Beat egg whites until stiff. Gently fold them into the yolks.

In a large, heavy skillet, over low heat, melt the butter or margarine. Pour the beaten eggs into the skillet and cook until omelet rises a bit and is crusty on the bottom. Spread the jam on one half of it and gently fold the other half over with a spatula, being careful not to break it. (Unlike other omelets with bulky fillings, this one is relatively easy to fold over without using a second pan.) Cook for another minute, then carefully place on a warm platter. Sprinkle with confectioner's sugar and place fresh berries on and around the omelet.

Serves 4

CHICKEN LIVER OMELET

½ pound chicken livers
1 tablespoon flour
2 tablespoons butter or margarine
White pepper, to taste
Salt, to taste
⅛ cup chopped fresh parsley
¼ cup chicken stock
6 eggs

Dip the chicken livers in flour and shake off any excess. Melt 1 tablespoon of the butter in a skillet over medium heat. Sauté the chicken livers for 3 minutes. Sprinkle with white pepper, salt, and parsley. (You may want to add a little more butter to make them really crispy.) Add the chicken stock and flip the livers around to coat well. Remove from heat. Drain, reserving the sauce. Set aside.

Using 6 eggs, make an omelet (see page 46). When one side is crusty, add drained chicken livers and flip into the other pan. When done, remove from pan and fold onto a plate. Spoon remaining sauce over the omelet. Serve immediately.

Serves 2

Hint: Remember to ask your guests how they like their chicken livers cooked. I think medium-rare is best, but allow your guests to decide for themselves.

UN-NOUVELLE MUSHROOM OMELET

  2 *tablespoons sweet butter or margarine*
¼ *cup sliced fresh mushrooms*
   Pinch of white pepper
⅛ *cup chopped fresh parsley*
  3 *eggs*
   Hollandaise Sauce (see page 168)

Melt 1 tablespoon butter in a skillet, over medium heat, and sauté the mushrooms with pepper and parsley until they are barely cooked or until all the mushroom juice has disappeared. Set aside.

Make a 3-egg omelet (see page 46). Place mushroom mixture on top.

In another skillet, melt the other tablespoon of butter or margarine. When bottom of omelet is crusty, flip it over carefully into the second skillet and cook to seal the filling, about 1 to 2 minutes.

Remove from heat. Place on a serving plate and cover with hollandaise sauce.

Serves 1

Hint: Wash and dry mushrooms quickly. *Never* let them soak in water as they will soak *in* water and then release it when cooked. You will end up with a soggy, soupy omelet.

JAMES GARNER OMELET

  2 *tablespoons butter or margarine*
½ *cup sliced fresh mushrooms (try unusual mushrooms like*
   oyster, chanterelle, or morel)
¼ *cup cooked corn*
½ *cup Tomato Sauce (see page 170)*
  3 *eggs*

In a skillet, over medium heat, melt 1 tablespoon of butter or margarine and sauté the mushrooms and corn until light brown. Stir in the tomato sauce.

In another skillet, melt 1 tablespoon butter and make a 3-egg omelet (see page 46).

Pour the mushroom mixture onto the omelet. When bottom is crusty, turn into the other skillet and cook 1 more minute. This omelet should be soft inside.

Serves 1

Hint: Jim does love this omelet! This was also a favorite of mine when I lived in Bermuda. I used to garnish it with a native fruit called "strawberry banana." So delicious!

JANET'S BLUE CHEESE OMELET

> 3 *eggs*
> 2 *teaspoons butter or margarine*
> ¼ *cup crumbled blue cheese*
> ⅛ *cup chopped scallions*
> ½ *cup small pieces of matzo*

Beat the eggs. Melt 1 teaspoon butter or margarine in a skillet over medium heat. Add the eggs. Sprinkle with blue cheese and scallions. Add the broken matzo and cook until the bottom of the omelet is brown.

In another skillet, melt the other teaspoon of butter or margarine. Turn the omelet into this skillet. Cook until brown. Serve with strawberries or other fresh fruit.

Serves 1

TUNA FISH OMELET

1 *6-ounce can solid white, water-packed tuna*
¼ *cup chopped onion*
1 *tablespoon Mayonnaise (see page 173)*
⅛ *cup chopped fresh parsley*
6 *eggs*
2 *tablespoons butter or margarine*

Drain the tuna. In the food processor, using the steel blade, blend with the onion, mayonnaise, and parsley. Set aside.

In a small pan, heat the tuna mixture over a very low flame. Barely heat, or it will get oily and break apart. Melt butter in a skillet over low heat. Make a 6-egg omelet (see page 46). Place the tuna in the omelet, cook until bottom is crusty, and turn over into second pan. Cook until done. Serve with boiled red potatoes and garnish with fresh parsley.

Serves 2

SPINACH OMELET

3 *eggs*
2 *tablespoons butter or margarine*
1 *cup chopped fresh spinach leaves*
½ *cup grated Swiss cheese*
1 *tablespoon sour cream*
  Pinch of grated nutmeg

Make a 3-egg omelet (see page 46). While the bottom is browning, sprinkle the spinach leaves, cheese, sour cream, and nutmeg on top. When the bottom is crusty, turn over into another pan and cook until done.

Serve with sliced tomatoes, fresh strawberries, or a steamed vegetable as garnish.

Serves 1

Hint: Spinach leaves love to hide dirt. You must wash them well— sometimes again and again. Dry in paper towels or in a salad spinner. Cut off the stems before using.

HEAVEN'S GATE OMELET

I named this "Heaven's Gate" because I figured it's what I'll be served when I enter the Pearly Gates. It is so easy—not to get into Heaven's Gate, but to make this omelet!

1   tablespoon butter or margarine
3   eggs
2   tablespoons sour cream
¼   cup chopped onion
1 to 2   ounces Malossal Iranian caviar

Melt the butter or margarine in a skillet, over low heat. Beat the eggs and pour them into the skillet. When the bottom is crusty, fold in half and remove to a warm serving plate.

Place sour cream, chopped onion, and caviar on top of the omelet. Serve with toasted sour-dough bread and cold aquavit.

Serves 1 very happy person

Hint: You can use any caviar you like. Malossal is special, but you can even use salmon roe.

STRAWBERRY AND BANANA OMELET

6 to 8 *fresh strawberries*
    1 *whole banana, sliced thin*
    1 *tablespoon brown sugar*
      Dash of vanilla
      Pinch of ground cinnamon
    2 *tablespoons butter or margarine*
      Juice of 1 lemon or lime
    3 *eggs*
    1 *teaspoon confectioner's sugar*
    1 *tablespoon sour cream*
   ½ *cup sliced fresh berries*

Wash the strawberries and cut in half. Place them in a skillet with the banana, brown sugar, vanilla, cinnamon, 1 tablespoon butter or margarine, and lemon or lime juice. Sauté over medium heat until a brown syrup forms.

Beat the eggs. Melt 1 tablespoon butter or margarine in a skillet, over low heat, and cook eggs until bottom is brown. Fill with strawberry mixture. Fold the omelet over and remove to serving plate (or use my two-pan method, see page 46). Top with confectioner's sugar, sour cream, and sliced fresh berries.

Serves 1

Hint: Use *fresh* strawberries—their sweetness is important. The bananas should be ripe but quite firm, otherwise you'll make banana mush.

KITCHEN SINK OMELET

On a day when you wonder "What's to eat?" think Kitchen Sink Omelet. You probably have milk, eggs, bread, and some type of fruit or vegetable in the refrigerator or pantry. You can concoct an omelet with just about anything you have on hand.

> *Whatever you find in your refrigerator, chopped*
> *Any seasonings you like, to taste*
> 3 *tablespoons butter or margarine*
> 3 *eggs*

Take the ingredients you have chosen, chop up those that require it, season, and sauté in a skillet with 1 tablespoon melted butter.

In another skillet, melt 1 tablespoon butter or margarine. Beat the eggs and pour them into the skillet. Cook the omelet until bottom is brown. Add the filling, flip into another skillet in which you have melted 1 tablespoon butter or margarine, and cook 1 minute more.

Remove from heat and serve immediately.

Serves 1

POACHED EGGS

POACHED EGGS

1 *tablespoon butter or margarine*
1 *egg*
   Boiling water
   Salt

Melt the butter or margarine in a small saucepan. Add enough slightly salted boiling water to fill pan twice the depth of an egg. Bring to a boil.

Carefully break 1 egg into a small bowl. With a wooden spoon, swiftly swirl the boiling water until it forms a well. Gently drop the egg into the center of the well. (The swirling water will give the egg a well-rounded shape.) Reduce heat and simmer 2 minutes. Remove from heat and let stand for 2 minutes or until the white is firm and the yolk still soft.

Remove the egg with a skimmer and serve immediately. If poaching several eggs, use a pan large enough to avoid crowding.

Serves 1

Hint: If you are not using the egg immediately, plunge it into a bowl of cold water. This will stop the cooking process. To reheat egg, carefully place in hot, not boiling, water (enough to cover egg) and heat over low flame for about 1 minute.

Another Hint: If you have trouble poaching eggs, add 1 teaspoon vinegar to the water. It will help keep the whites from disintegrating. Poach only the freshest eggs as the white of a stale egg will spread all over the pan.

BANANA DELIGHT WITH EGGS

1 tablespoon butter or margarine
2 bananas, firm but not green, sliced lengthwise
4 slices bacon, broiled or baked crisp
4 eggs, poached (see page 58)
1 teaspoon chopped fresh parsley
1 medium tomato, diced
½ teaspoon ground cinnamon

In a skillet, over medium heat, melt the butter or margarine. Sauté the bananas until golden brown. Divide the bananas onto two serving plates. Top each serving with 2 slices of bacon, 2 poached eggs, ½ teaspoon chopped parsley, ½ diced tomato, and ¼ teaspoon ground cinnamon. Serve immediately.

Serves 2

Hint: Be certain that the bacon is crisp so that there isn't any extra oil. The eggs should be poached to medium-soft.

EGGS COQUETTE

Butter
2 eggs
2 slices bacon, sausage, or ham
2 slices toast

Preheat oven to 375°.

Butter two individual soufflé dishes. Break 1 egg into each. Place the soufflé dishes in a glass baking dish. Fill baking dish with enough water to surround soufflé dishes halfway. Cover. Put the baking dish with the soufflé dishes in the preheated oven and bake for 5 minutes. While the eggs are cooking, brown the meat in a skillet. Keep your eyes on the eggs—they should be soft in the center, with the whites slightly crusty.

On a serving plate, put 2 slices of toast, then place meat on top. Serve the eggs in their dishes.

Serves 1

BENEDICTINE EGGS

½ *pound dried codfish*
½ *tablespoon butter or margarine*
⅛ *cup chopped fresh parsley*
2 *eggs, poached*
½ *cup White Sauce (see page 171)*
  Pinch of freshly ground pepper

Soak the codfish in water overnight, covered, to get rid of most of the salt. Drain. Purée in a food processor with the butter and parsley.

Preheat oven to 350°.

Heat the puréed codfish in a 350° oven for 10 minutes. Divide in half onto serving plates. Place a poached egg on each. Pour equal portions of white sauce on top. Garnish with freshly ground pepper or cracked peppercorns.

Serves 2

Hint: If you're lucky enough to have truffles in your Perfect Pantry, throw them on the white sauce. They will add the perfect touch.

MY DAD'S EGGS FROM HEAVEN

Wouldn't you like to know how these eggs got their name? Let's just say that they are great for nursing a hangover.

6 *slices bread*
3 *tablespoons butter or margarine*
12 *oysters, shucked*
6 *slices crisp bacon*
6 *anchovy fillets*
6 *eggs, poached*
  Cajun Spice (see page 172)
1 *tablespoon chopped fresh parsley*
1 *pound Brie*

Fry the bread in 2 tablespoons butter until it is crisp. Keep warm in oven (or toaster oven) but do not let it get soggy.

Using the same skillet, sauté the oysters gently in 1 tablespoon butter or margarine, 1 minute on each side. Put a slice of toast on each of six serving plates and divide the oysters among them. Place 1 piece of bacon on each slice of toast. Place an anchovy fillet on top. Gently cover with 1 poached egg. Sprinkle with Cajun spice and chopped parsley. Place a slice of Brie on top, then heat under the broiler for about 1 minute or until cheese is soft but not browned. Serve immediately.

Serves 6

Hint: A bottle of Guinness or other imported cold beer served with this will ensure that you'll be hangover free.

SCULLY'S EGGS BENEDICT WITH CHEESE AND BACON

2 *eggs*
1 *English muffin, cut in half*
  Butter or margarine
  Freshly grated nutmeg, to taste
2 *slices each of Monterey Jack, cheddar, and Swiss cheese*
1 *tablespoon grated Parmesan cheese*
4 *slices crisp bacon (or Canadian bacon)*

Preheat oven to Broil.

Poach the eggs (see page 58). While they are cooking, toast the muffin halves. When toasted, spread with butter or margarine. Shake some nutmeg on each muffin half and place a poached egg on top. Cover with 1 slice of each cheese. Sprinkle on grated Parmesan and place under the broiler until the cheeses are melted. Remove from broiler. Place 2 slices crisply cooked bacon across the top of each muffin half. Serve immediately.

Serves 2

Hint: Notice that I make eggs Benedict without hollandaise sauce. This recipe came about when I ran out of hollandaise at the restaurant and used the cheeses instead. (I've always got plenty of cheese on hand.) People liked it, so I kept on making it that way. But, of course, you can serve it with hollandaise sauce if you wish.

POACHED EGGS GOURMET

Or the Once-a-Year Ultimate Breakfast for One;
or How to Spoil Yourself Totally

> 2 *slices thin white toast (preferably from homemade bread)*
> 2 *slices goose liver pâté*
> 3 *truffles, chopped*
> 2 *eggs, poached*
>   *Pepper, to taste*

Place 1 slice of toast on each of two serving plates. Lay the pâté on the toast. Sprinkle with truffles. Cover with a poached egg. Top with fresh, cracked pepper. Serve immediately.

Fabulous!

Serves 2

Hint: Serve with Cristal champagne.

EGGS INDIAN

> 8 *eggs*
> 4 *English muffins, sliced and toasted*
> 4 *cups Curry Sauce*
> 2 *bananas, sliced*
> 2 *teaspoons chopped fresh cilantro or*
> 3 *tablespoons slivered almonds (optional)*

Poach the eggs (see page 58). Place 2 muffin halves on each of four plates. Center a poached egg on each. Cover with Curry Sauce. Lay banana slices on top and sprinkle with chopped cilantro or slivered almonds.

Serves 4

Hint: Serve with a variety of chutneys on the side.

Curry Sauce

> 2 *tablespoons butter or margarine*
> 1 *tablespoon flour*
>   *Pinch of each:*
>   *Brown sugar*
>   *Curry powder*
>   *Cumin powder*
>   *Ground ginger*
> ½ *cup half-and-half*

Melt butter in a small saucepan over medium heat. Stir in flour. Add sugar and spices. Cook, stirring constantly, for 2 to 3 minutes, then gradually add half-and-half. Keep stirring until thick. Set aside but keep warm.

RUSSIAN EGGS (EGGS MOSCOVITE)

Or the Once-Every-Other-Year Breakfast;
or the Day I Signed My New Movie Deal Breakfast;
or the Morning After the Wedding Breakfast

> 2 *slices white toast*
> 2 *eggs, poached*
> 4 *tablespoons Hollandaise Sauce (see page 168)*
> 1 *ounce Beluga or Sevruga caviar*

Place 1 slice of toast on each of two serving plates. Place a poached egg on each and cover with 2 tablespoons hollandaise sauce. Top with caviar.

Serve with ice-cold vodka or aquavit.

Serves 2

Hint: Be prepared to give up half of everything you own after eating this—you'll be in such a great mood! Don't say I didn't warn you!

EGGS FLORENTINE

4 *eggs*
1 *cup cooked chopped fresh spinach*
¼ *teaspoon ground nutmeg*
2 *tablespoons sweet butter or margarine, melted*
1 *recipe Cheddar Sauce*
1 *tablespoon grated Parmesan cheese*
¼ *cup bread crumbs ·*

Preheat oven to Broil.

Poach the eggs (see page 58) and set aside. Mix the spinach with nutmeg and melted butter. Heat through in a microwave or in a small saucepan, quickly, over low heat.

Divide the spinach onto the centers of two serving plates. Place two poached eggs on top of each portion and cover with Cheddar Sauce. Sprinkle with grated Parmesan cheese and bread crumbs. Place under the broiler for a couple of seconds to heat through. Remove from broiler and serve immediately.

Cheddar Sauce

⅛ *cup butter*
⅛ *cup flour*
½ *cup shredded cheddar cheese*
¼ *cup half-and-half*

In a small saucepan, over low heat, melt the butter. Stir in the flour. When well blended, add the cheese and half-and-half. Cook, whisking constantly, over medium heat until thick.

Serves 2

HARD-BOILED EGGS

CREAMED EGGS WITH MUSHROOMS

½ cup half-and-half
¾ cup cream cheese, softened
2 cups grated cheddar cheese
1 cup sautéed mushrooms, drained
4 slices white toast
4 hard-boiled eggs, sliced

Scald the half-and-half in the top of a double boiler over hot water. Add the cheese and mushrooms. Cook, stirring constantly, until smooth. Place 1 slice of toast on each of four serving plates. Cover each with 1 sliced hard-boiled egg and cheese sauce. Garnish with steamed asparagus, grilled tomato, or fresh string beans.

Serves 4

Hint: If you want to add meat to this dish, dice some ham and sprinkle over the top of each serving.

STUFFED EGGS WITH CRAB MEAT

10 hard-boiled eggs
1 tablespoon dry mustard
½ teaspoon salt
1 cup flaked crab meat
1 cup finely chopped celery
2 tablespoons finely chopped green pepper
¾ cup Mayonnaise (see page 173)
Paprika for garnish

Cut the eggs into halves lengthwise and remove the yolks. Mash yolks into the remaining ingredients, except for paprika. When well blended, refill the whites and sprinkle with paprika.

Makes 20 stuffed eggs

EGGS DIABLO

8 hard-boiled eggs, sliced
8 slices buttered toast
1 cup tomato catsup
½ cup chili sauce
2 tablespoons Worcestershire sauce
1 tablespoon butter or margarine
1½ tablespoons prepared mustard
1 tablespoon wine vinegar
½ teaspoon salt
½ teaspoon pepper

Place 1 sliced hard-boiled egg on top of each piece of toast. Place each on a serving plate.

In a small saucepan, combine remaining ingredients and cook, stirring constantly, until well blended. When sauce is done, pour equal portions over each slice of toast with egg. Serve immediately.

Serves 8

EGGS BAVARIAN STYLE

4 tablespoons sweet butter or margarine
4 tablespoons flour
1 cup milk
½ teaspoon salt
½ teaspoon paprika
⅛ teaspoon pepper
8 hard-boiled eggs
½ cup bread crumbs

In a skillet, over medium heat, melt 2 tablespoons butter. Blend in the flour. When well blended, add the milk and seasonings. Cook, stirring constantly, until thick. Remove from heat and set aside.

Dip the hard-boiled eggs into the sauce, then roll the eggs in bread crumbs to coat. Melt the remaining 2 tablespoons of butter in the skillet over medium heat and fry eggs until brown on all sides. Drain on paper towels. Serve immediately.

Serves 8

Variation: Cut the hard-boiled eggs in half lengthwise. Remove the yolks. Make a filling by mixing the yolks with 2 tablespoons finely minced green pepper and 2 tablespoons grated sharp cheese. Refill the whites and fasten the halves together with toothpicks. Prepare as above.

Hint: Serve with Tomato Sauce (see page 170).

EGGS CROQUETTE

> 3 *tablespoons butter or margarine*
> 3 *tablespoons flour*
> ¾ *cup milk*
>   *Pinch of salt*
>   *Pinch of paprika*
> 4 *hard-boiled eggs, chopped*
> 2 *cups mashed potatoes*
> ½ *cup bread or cracker crumbs*
> 1 *egg, beaten*
> 3 *cups peanut oil for deep frying*

Melt the butter or margarine in the top half of a double boiler over boiling water. Add the flour and stir until well blended. Stir in the milk and seasonings and cook over medium heat until thick. Remove from heat and stir in the hard-boiled eggs. Mix into the mashed potatoes. Set aside to cool.

When the mixture is cold, shape into 3-inch-long croquettes. Roll in crumbs and dip into beaten egg.

In a deep, heavy saucepan or deep-fat fryer, heat the oil (1 inch deep or more) until very hot. Fry the croquettes until they are golden brown—about 3 to 4 minutes. Remove from heat. Drain and serve immediately with the sauce of your choice.

Serves 2

Hint: Be sure that the oil is very fresh.

SCOTCH EGGS

6 *hard-boiled eggs, peeled and left whole*
2 *tablespoons hot milk*
12 *ounces uncooked Homemade Sausage meat (see page 128)*
¼ *cup bread crumbs*
1 *teaspoon finely minced onion*
1 *tablespoon finely minced fresh parsley*
2 *cups safflower oil*
6 *pieces fried bread (sour dough or French)*
  English mustard

Roll the hard-boiled eggs in the milk.

Divide the sausage meat into six portions. Mix the bread crumbs, onion, and parsley together. Roll sausage around each egg and dip into the bread crumbs and parsley. Set aside.

Heat the oil in a deep pot until very hot. Fry the eggs until the meat is cooked and well browned, about 5 to 7 minutes. When done, drain on paper towels. Let cool. Cut in half and serve on fried bread. Garnish with English mustard.

Serves 6

Hint: Serve with a green salad.

HAM AND EGG CROQUETTES

1 *can cream of mushroom soup*
8 *hard-boiled eggs, chopped*
1 *teaspoon salt*
½ *teaspoon Worcestershire sauce*
½ *teaspoon mustard*
1½ *cups chopped cooked ham*
2½ *cups bread crumbs*
1 *egg, beaten with 2 tablespoons water*
½ *cup safflower oil*

In a saucepan, over medium heat, heat the mushroom soup. Stir in eggs, salt, Worcestershire sauce, mustard, ham, and 1½ cups bread crumbs. Cook for 5 minutes. Remove from heat and refrigerate for 10 minutes.

Shape into croquettes. Roll in the remaining 1 cup of bread crumbs to coat, dip into the beaten egg, and roll in the crumbs again. Set aside.

Heat the oil in a skillet over medium heat. Fry the croquettes for 3 to 5 minutes, or until golden brown. Drain on paper towels and serve immediately with Tarragon Sauce (see page 169), Tomato Sauce (see page 170), or, if you really want to go to town, Hollandaise Sauce (see page 168).

Serves 4

Hint: Make your own bread crumbs by toasting old bread and grinding it in the food processor.

SCRAMBLED EGGS

EGGS NORMA

2 *tablespoons butter or margarine*
3 *eggs*
   Dash of vinegar or fresh lemon juice
1 *tablespoon capers*
⅛ *cup chopped fresh parsley*
2 *slices French bread, toasted*

Melt 1 tablespoon of the butter or margarine in a skillet over medium heat. Scramble the eggs. In another skillet, melt 1 tablespoon butter or margarine. Let it get very brown, almost burned. Add a dash of vinegar or lemon juice, capers, and chopped parsley. Stir to coat. Remove from heat.

Place the toasted French bread on a serving plate. Cover with eggs, then coat with the caper mixture. Serve immediately.

Serves 1

EGGS RUE MADELEINE

This is a variation of the Chicken Liver Omelet which is very popular in Europe.

3 *tablespoons butter or margarine*
3 *eggs*
½ *pound chicken livers*
   Flour
¼ *cup chopped fresh parsley*
1 *clove garlic, mashed*
¼ *cup chopped onion*
¼ *cup Easy Gravy (see page 166)*
2 *slices toast*

In a skillet, over medium heat, melt 1 tablespoon butter or margarine. Scramble the eggs. Set aside.

In another skillet, melt 2 tablespoons butter. Dip chicken livers in flour to coat. Fry, stirring frequently, until slightly crisp. Add parsley, garlic, and onion. Sauté for 5 minutes. Stir in brown sauce. Place the scrambled eggs on a plate and immediately spoon the chicken livers on top. Serve with toast.

Serves 1 to 2

Hint: Drink Pernod over ice while devouring this heavenly dish!

EGGS RANCHERO

2 *flour tortillas*
1 *tablespoon butter or margarine*
4 *eggs*
1 *small onion, peeled, sliced, and grilled*
1 *medium tomato, sliced*
  Salsa (see page 169)
½ *cup grated Swiss, cheddar, or Mexican Jack cheese*
2 *jalapeño peppers*
1 *cup enchilada sauce (commercially made is fine; op-tional)*

Preheat oven to 350°.

Heat the tortillas in the oven until they are soft and pliable.

In a skillet, over medium heat, melt the butter or margarine. Beat the eggs, pour into the skillet, and scramble. Place 2 scrambled eggs on each tortilla. Garnish each plate with grilled onions, sliced tomato, salsa, cheese, and peppers. You can pour some enchilada sauce over it all, if you wish. Serve immediately.

Serves 2

Variation: Place the cheese on top of the tortilla and broil to melt it onto the tortilla. Then place the eggs on top and finish with the remaining garnishes.

Hint: This is also tasty with 2 slices of avocado on each tortilla. What a treat! One grilled ortega chili will also add zest to the eggs.

KIPPERS AND EGGS

1 *smoked Scotch kipper*
1 *tablespoon sweet butter or margarine*
3 *eggs*
2 *slices wheat toast*
1 *tablespoon sour cream*
1 *onion slice*

Preheat oven to Broil.

Broil kipper about 5 minutes under high heat. Pull out the breast bone and the back skin with your fingers. You will have a fillet of kipper.

In a skillet, over medium heat, melt the butter or margarine. Scramble the eggs. Add the kipper and cook for 1 minute. Serve immediately, garnished with wheat toast, sour cream, and an onion slice.

Serves 1

EGGS IN POTATO BOATS

4 *medium baking potatoes, washed well*
2 *tablespoons butter or margarine*
2 *tablespoons chopped fresh chives*
½ *teaspoon salt*
½ *teaspoon freshly ground black pepper*
   Pinch of grated nutmeg
¼ *cup half-and-half*
6 *eggs, beaten*
   Iranian caviar (optional)

Preheat oven to 425°.

Prick washed potatoes with a fork. Place on a metal baking pan and bake for 1 hour.

Remove from oven, slice in half lengthwise, and scoop out the pulp, being careful not to damage skins. Set skins aside.

In the food processor, using the steel blade, blend the potato pulp with 1 tablespoon margarine. Remove to a mixing bowl and add chives, salt, pepper, and nutmeg. Slowly pour in the half-and-half, beating constantly with a wooden spoon.

In a skillet, over medium heat, melt 1 tablespoon butter or margarine. Scramble the eggs. Stuff the baked skins with the mashed potato mixture and top with scrambled eggs. Place stuffed potatoes on a baking dish and bake at 425° for 5 to 7 minutes or until heated through. Top each with a teaspoon of caviar and serve immediately.

Serves 4

Hint: Try the caviar! It adds a special touch to this dish, and if you are making it for only four people, it won't cost too much.

SCRAMBLED EGGS WITH MARIGOLDS

Flower child Renée Golden, my attorney, thinks it is still 1962. She bakes her own bread, makes her own chips, listens to Peter, Paul, and Mary, and grows herbs and flowers in her carefully tended garden. This is her attempt to convert me!

> 4 *eggs*
> 4 *tablespoons milk*
> ⅛ *teaspoon salt*
>   *Pinch of pepper*
>   *Pinch of grated nutmeg*
> 1 *tablespoon butter or margarine*
> 2 *washed and chopped marigold flowers (no stems)*
>   *Pumpernickel toast*

Beat together the eggs, milk, salt, pepper, and nutmeg. Melt the butter or margarine in a skillet over medium heat. Scramble the eggs. While still wet, add the marigolds. Keep cooking until the eggs are well scrambled.

Serve immediately on pumpernickel toast and garnish with more fresh marigolds.

Serves 2

VEAL OR LAMB KIDNEYS AND EGGS

½ *pound veal or lamb kidneys*
2 *tablespoons plus 1 teaspoon butter or margarine*
½ *cup chopped onion*
3 *eggs, beaten*
2 *slices toast*
   Salt and pepper, to taste

Wash the kidneys. Dry with paper towels. Trim kidneys of all fat and cut into small pieces. In a skillet, over medium heat, melt 2 tablespoons butter or margarine. Lower heat and sauté kidneys, covered, stirring frequently, for 15 minutes or until nicely browned.

In another skillet, over low heat, melt 1 teaspoon butter or margarine. Sauté the onion until soft and transparent. Pour in the eggs and scramble.

Place the toast on a serving plate. Put the scrambled eggs on the toast and cover with sautéed kidneys. Season with salt and pepper to taste. Serve immediately.

Serves 1

Hint: Veal kidneys are usually eaten medium-rare to medium and do taste better that way. So don't overcook them! Lamb kidneys will take a few minutes longer to cook through.

SCRAMBLED EGGS WITH MATZOS

6 *matzos*
5 *cups boiling water*
12 *eggs*
   Salt, to taste
   White pepper, to taste
1 *tablespoon sweet butter or margarine*

Crumble matzos into a large bowl. Add boiling water. Cover the bowl and let the matzos soak for about 5 minutes. Drain and squeeze water out of matzos. Set aside.

Beat the eggs. Add salt and pepper to taste. Stir in matzos. Melt butter in a large skillet over medium heat. Pour in the matzo-egg mixture. You now have an option—you can either prepare this as you would scrambled eggs or you can let it cook on the bottom (get it crusty!) and then flip it into another pan as you would to make an omelet. The latter will result in a more pancake-like dish. Serve with chopped fresh parsley or maple syrup.

Serves 4

Hint: You can soak the matzo in Chicken Stock (see page 115) and fry in chicken fat for a richer taste.

SCRAMBLED EGGS ITALIAN

>   2 *tablespoons olive oil*
> 12 *eggs*
>   1 *tablespoon chopped fresh basil*
>   1 *tablespoon grated fresh Parmesan cheese*
>   *Garlic Bread*

Heat olive oil in a heavy skillet over medium heat until very hot. Beat the eggs with the basil and cheese. Scramble them quickly and lightly and serve on slices of toasted Italian garlic bread.

Serves 4

Garlic Bread

>   1 *long Italian bread, sliced*

For each slice, you will need:

>   1 *tablespoon sweet butter or margarine*
> ½ *teaspoon garlic, minced*

For each slice you will be preparing, melt 1 tablespoon butter or margarine in a skillet over medium heat. Add ½ teaspoon garlic per slice and sauté for 30 seconds. Do not let it burn. Remove from heat and brush garlic-butter on each slice of bread. Toast under broiler or in toaster oven until brown, making sure not to burn. Serve immediately.

EGGS TONI BROTMAN

1 *tablespoon sweet butter or margarine*
3 *eggs*
¼ *pound ground prime sirloin*
¼ *cup finely chopped onion*
⅛ *cup chopped green pepper*
⅛ *cup chopped mushrooms*
1 *cup spinach leaves, stems removed*
¼ *cup grated cheddar cheese*
3 *small boiled potatoes*

In a skillet, over medium heat, melt the butter or margarine. Scramble the eggs. Set aside.

In another skillet, sauté the meat (don't add butter—there will be enough fat in the meat) with the onion, pepper, mushrooms, and spinach leaves until the meat is brown and the other ingredients soft. Drain off any excess fat. Quickly stir in the scrambled eggs. Add the cheddar cheese. Sauté for another minute. Serve immediately with boiled potatoes on the side.

Serves 1

Hint: You can cook the meat as long as you like, but generally it is better rare to medium-rare. The more you cook it, the more it dries out. This dish tastes better when it is moist.

Another Hint: Serve with thin rye toast or a crisp tortilla so you can scoop up the good stuff.

MEXICAN EGGS

4 *tablespoons butter or margarine*
4 *tomatoes, peeled and chopped*
1 *clove elephant garlic, minced*
1 *small onion, finely chopped*
2 *sweet green peppers, chopped*
8 *tortillas*
8 *eggs*
4 *slices Monterey Jack cheese*
2 *ripe avocados, mashed*

Preheat oven to 300°.

In a small saucepan, over medium heat, melt 1 tablespoon butter or margarine. Cook the tomatoes, garlic, and onion for 15 minutes or until thick. Set aside.

In a skillet, over medium heat, melt 1 tablespoon butter or margarine. Fry the peppers until soft. Set aside.

Heat the tortillas in 300° oven. Beat the eggs. Melt 2 tablespoons butter in a skillet, over low heat. Scramble the eggs. When eggs are done, place 2 eggs on each of 4 tortillas. Cover each with a slice of cheese and equal portions of fried pepper and mashed avocado. Cover with warm tomato mixture and serve. Use the other heated tortillas for scooping.

Serves 4

Hint: Don't peel garlic with a paring knife. Put the clove on a wooden chopping block and press hard with a wooden spoon or the side of a chopping knife. The skin will easily slide off.

ONIONS AND EGGS

I love the smell of onions cooking. I often leave my kitchen door open so my customers can also enjoy the aroma. But when they insist on coming into the kitchen, I have to close the door! So, here is my famous Onions and Eggs recipe so you can have that wonderful smell all to yourselves.

4 *sweet onions (Maui are great), sliced thin*
2 *tablespoons butter or margarine*
6 *eggs, beaten*
    Salt and pepper, to taste (optional)

Make certain the onions are sliced very thin. Separate into rings. In a skillet, over medium heat, melt the butter or margarine. Add the onions. Lower heat and cook, stirring frequently, for at least 30 minutes. The onions should be brown and nearly glazed. When they are nicely brown, pour in the eggs. Add salt and pepper to taste, and scramble.

Serve with toast and sliced beefsteak tomatoes.

Serves 2

Hint: Remember that the sweeter the onion, the better the taste of this dish. Maui onions, when available, are expensive but worth it; they really make a difference in the taste. The onions make this a sweet dish, so I don't recommend salting or peppering the eggs. But some people can't eat eggs unless they are seasoned—so go ahead, if you must.

TORTILLA WAFFLES

This recipe is a lot of fun to make, so invite your lucky guests to watch or, better yet, to help. Just make the first one, keep it warm, and then make the second.

2 *eggs*
8 *cocktail tortillas (the small ones, either corn or flour)*
2 *tablespoons butter or margarine*
4 *eggs, scrambled*
4 *tablespoons Salsa (see page 169)*
2 *tablespoons enchilada sauce*
½ *avocado, sliced*
1 *cup grated Monterey Jack cheese*
  Sour cream, for garnish
2 *tablespoons chopped raw onions, for garnish*

Preheat oven to Broil.

Beat the eggs. Dip the tortillas one by one into the egg. Melt the butter or margarine in a small skillet over medium heat. Fry the dipped tortillas until they are crisp and golden brown. Remove from heat and drain on paper towel.

Place one tortilla on an ovenproof plate. Place half the scrambled eggs on top. Cover with another tortilla. Put a tablespoon each of salsa and enchilada sauce on top of the tortilla, and then add another tortilla. Top with half of the sliced avocado, 1 tablespoon salsa, and another tortilla. Top with ½ cup grated Monterey Jack cheese. Put the plate aside. With remaining ingredients, make the second tortilla waffle. When complete, place under the broiler until the cheese has melted and run down the sides. Be sure you have enough cheese on top so that the tortilla does not burn.

Garnish with sour cream and chopped onion. Serve immediately. Add a glass of sangria or a margarita and you've got it made!

Serves 2

Hint: You may also wish to offer your guests extra sliced avocado and salsa.

FRIED EGGS

FRIED TORTILLAS AND EGGS

3 *tortillas*
2 *eggs, fried*
2 *tablespoons butter or margarine*
1 *ounce tequila or sherry*
⅛ *cup chopped fresh cilantro*
½ *avocado, sliced*
1 *small tomato, diced*
1 *small onion, diced*
1 *jalapeño pepper, diced*

Heat 2 tortillas over the stove. (Simply place on the burner, over low heat, until sides curl up and are slightly brown and crisp.) Arrange on a serving plate, and place 1 fried egg on top of each cooked tortilla.

In a small saucepan, over medium heat, melt the butter or margarine. Stir in the tequila or sherry. Bring to a boil and quickly pour over the eggs. Serve immediately with cilantro, avocado, tomato, onion, and pepper on top or on the side. Serve a soft tortilla as a scoop.

Serves 1

PANCAKES

ENGLISH PANCAKES

¾ *cup all-purpose flour*
⅓ *teaspoon salt*
2 *eggs*
2 *cups milk*
1 *tablespoon butter*
1 *teaspoon confectioner's sugar*
1 *teaspoon fresh lemon juice*

Sift the flour and salt into a bowl. Using a wooden spoon, make a hole in the center and drop in the eggs. Gradually stir in half the milk. Beat well. Keep adding milk and beating until the liquid is absorbed. Let stand, covered, in a cool place for about an hour.

When you are ready to make the pancakes, pour and scrape all the batter into a jug or pitcher.

Melt butter in a small skillet over medium heat. Heat until a faint blue smoke rises. Pour in enough batter to cover the bottom of the pan with a thin layer, as if making crepes. Reduce heat and cook until the bottom is golden. Turn and cook until the other side is brown. Remove from heat.

Place the pancake on a serving plate, sprinkle with confectioner's sugar and a little lemon juice. Or you can place some jam or sour cream in the center, roll up, and sprinkle with confectioner's sugar and lemon juice. Serve immediately.

Serves 2 to 4

Hint: Serve one guest at a time while making these pancakes, as they are best very hot.

RICOTTA PANCAKES

1 15-ounce container ricotta cheese
4 eggs
⅓ cup sifted all-purpose flour
2 tablespoons butter or margarine, melted
2 tablespoons sugar
1 teaspoon vanilla
½ cup butter or margarine
2 cups nonfat plain yogurt, vanilla yogurt, or sour cream

In the food processor, using the steel blade, blend all ingredients, except the ½ cup butter and the yogurt, until smooth.

In a skillet, over low heat, melt 1 tablespoon butter or margarine, using the rest as needed. Use a soupspoon to ladle the batter into the skillet, making each pancake silver-dollar size. When the pancake is brown on one side (this happens quickly), turn over *just once* to finish cooking.

As you remove each pancake from the pan, put it on a hot plate to keep warm. If you have an electric hot plate, set it on Medium and put a metal or heatproof glass dish on it. Stack the pancakes on it and keep them covered with aluminum foil. It is important to keep them warm since you will be making at least 30 pancakes. When all pancakes are ready, place on a warm serving plate, top with yogurt, and serve immediately.

Serves 4 to 6

Hint: You can use almost anything as a topping: jam, maple syrup, fruit or fruit syrups—alone, or in combination with yogurt or sour cream.

Because these pancakes are already sweet (ricotta is a sweet cheese), they also taste great when a contrasting flavor is introduced—try topping with salmon roe or caviar and a dab of sour cream.

BANANA DREAM PANCAKES

3 *tablespoons sugar*
½ *teaspoon ground cinnamon*
   Pinch of grated nutmeg
   Pinch of salt
3 *ripe bananas, sliced thin*
2 *tablespoons fresh lemon juice*
1 *tablespoon banana liqueur (optional)*
1 *cup milk*
½ *cup presifted all-purpose flour*
2 *eggs, beaten*
¼ *cup butter or margarine*
2 *tablespoons confectioner's sugar (optional)*

Preheat oven to 350°.

Combine the sugar, cinnamon, nutmeg, and salt. Place the bananas in a bowl. Sprinkle on lemon juice and spiced sugar. If you are using banana liqueur, add now. Set aside.

In the food processor, using the steel blade, mix the milk, flour, and eggs to make a batter.

Melt 1 tablespoon of the butter or margarine in a skillet over medium heat, using the rest as needed. Make large, 10-inch diameter pancakes. (I sometimes use my crepe pan to make these.) And remember, turn the pancakes only once. Set aside.

When all the pancakes are done, fill each one with equal portions of banana mixture. Roll and put in a baking dish, flat side up. Dot with butter and bake for 10 minutes.

Serve immediately. For the gluttons among us, you can garnish with confectioner's sugar, sour cream or pure maple syrup. But remember—this dish is already sweet!

Serves 2 to 4

Hint: You can freeze these pancakes as you do crepes. Make the banana filling in the morning while the pancakes are defrosting.

OLD-FASHIONED BUTTERMILK PANCAKES

So easy to make, these are great to serve to unexpected breakfast guests.

>   1 *egg, beaten*
>   1 *cup buttermilk*
>   2 *tablespoons safflower oil*
>   1 *cup all-purpose flour*
>   1 *tablespoon sugar*
>   2 *teaspoons baking powder*
>   ½ *teaspoon baking soda*
>   ½ *teaspoon salt*

In a food processor, using the steel blade, combine the beaten egg, buttermilk, and oil. Blend the flour, sugar, baking powder, baking soda, and salt. Add to the egg mixture, beating until well blended.

Grease a large griddle. Pour in enough batter to make 6-inch pancakes. When pancake top is bubbly, flip over with a spatula and brown other side. *Turn only once.* Serve immediately with syrup, melted butter, or margarine.

Serves 4

Hint: You can use blended nonfat plain yogurt if you don't have buttermilk.

POTATO PANCAKES WITH APPLESAUCE
AND SOUR CREAM

Ben Rochelle, owner of Snow Chief (who ran in the Kentucky Derby), gave me this recipe some time ago. It is delicious!

>   6 *medium potatoes*
>   4 *eggs, separated*
>   ¼ *teaspoon baking powder*
>   1 *teaspoon salt*
>   1 *tablespoon flour*
>   2 *tablespoons grated onion*
>   *Chunky applesauce*
>   *Sour cream*

To prepare the potatoes: Peel, cover with cold water, and refrigerate for 12 hours. Drain. Grate the potatoes and squeeze out all extra liquid. Beat the egg yolks. Add to the grated potatoes. Stir in baking powder, salt, flour, and onion. Mix well.

Beat the egg whites until stiff and fold into the potatoes.

Heat a nonstick skillet until it is *very* hot. Drop the pancake batter, a tablespoon at a time, into the skillet. When the bottom of the pancake browns, turn over. Turn only once!

Serve with chunky applesauce and sour cream.

Serves 2 to 4

Hint: For an unusual flavor, sprinkle some caraway seeds on top before serving.

Another Hint: If you get caught without any applesauce in the pantry and haven't made your own, you can, if you have some apples on hand, make some at the last minute. Core and peel 4 to 6 apples, and chop them in the food processor with 1 teaspoon grated cinnamon and 1 teaspoon grated nutmeg. That's it—fresh, uncooked applesauce!

VARIATION POTATO PANCAKES

A last-minute alternative to "real" potato pancakes.

> 2 *cups grated freshly boiled potatoes (or a 12-ounce package frozen grated potatoes)*
> ¼ *cup finely chopped scallions*
> 1 *16-ounce package frozen pancake mix*
> *Pinch of salt*
> *Pinch of white pepper*
> ½ *cup sour cream*

Mix all ingredients, except sour cream, together. Grease and heat pancake griddle or nonstick skillet. Cook the pancakes, turning only once to brown.

Serve immediately with a dab of sour cream. You may also garnish with pure maple syrup and crisp bacon.

Serves 4

WHOLE-WHEAT PANCAKES

1½ *cups whole-wheat flour*
 3 *cups all-purpose flour*
 2 *tablespoons brown sugar*
 1 *tablespoon baking powder*
 ½ *teaspoon salt*
 3 *eggs, beaten*
 1 *cup milk*
 3 *tablespoons safflower oil or melted*
    butter or margarine

Thoroughly mix together the flours, sugar, baking powder, and salt. Beat the eggs, milk, and oil. Add to the dry ingredients, beating until well blended.

Grease a griddle or nonstick skillet and cook the pancakes, turning only once to brown.

Serve immediately with honey and/or maple syrup. I particularly love blueberry syrup on these.

Serves 4

Hint: You can add ½ cup mashed potatoes to the batter. This will make wonderfully light potato cakes.

FLUFFY YOGURT PANCAKES

  4 *eggs*
1¾ *cups all-purpose flour*
  2 *teaspoons baking powder*
  1 *tablespoon sugar*
  ½ *teaspoon salt*
  2 *cups nonfat plain yogurt*
  3 *tablespoons butter or margarine, melted*
  2 *tablespoons butter or margarine*

Separate the eggs. Beat the whites until stiff. Set aside.

In a mixing bowl, sift the flour, baking powder, sugar, and salt.

Beat the egg yolks, adding the yogurt while beating. Pour into flour and mix with a wooden spoon until blended. Stir in the melted butter or margarine. Carefully fold in the whites.

In a heavy skillet, over medium heat, melt the other 2 tablespoons butter or margarine. Ladle in enough batter to make small pancakes, about 4 inches in diameter. When they are brown on one side, turn them over to finish cooking.

Serve immediately with syrup or jam.

Serves 6

Hint: If you love yogurt, serve it on top of the pancakes also. Blend either plain or fruit-flavored yogurt in the food processor for 5 seconds and serve as a topping.

EASY BAKED APPLE PANCAKE

3 *apples, peeled, cored, and sliced*
Juice of 1 lemon
1 *tablespoon butter or margarine*
4 *eggs*
Pinch of grated nutmeg
½ *cup all-purpose flour*
½ *teaspoon salt*
½ *cup milk*
¼ *teaspoon vanilla*
2 *tablespoons butter or margarine*
1 *teaspoon confectioner's sugar*
½ *teaspoon fresh lemon juice*

Preheat oven to 400°.

Cover the apple slices with lemon juice. Melt butter in a skillet and gently, over a low flame, sauté the apples until they are soft and lightly browned. Set aside.

In the food processor, using the steel blade, beat the eggs with the nutmeg. Sift the flour and salt and add to the eggs, beating constantly. Gradually add the milk and continue blending until the batter is smooth. Stir in the vanilla.

In an ovenproof frying pan (or, if you have one, a round, metal pan for baking pancakes), melt 2 tablespoons butter or margarine. Pour batter into the pan and place apples in the middle.

Place in oven and bake for 15 minutes at 400°. Lower the oven temperature to 350° and bake for another 5 minutes or until the pancake rises and is fluffy. (Your oven temperature should be exact for this to work.)

Once you remove the pancake from the oven, work quickly so it doesn't get cold. Sprinkle with confectioner's sugar, a few drops of lemon juice, and serve immediately. (You can cut into wedges or scoop to serve.) It will be a great hit!

Serves 4

Hint: Use Pippin apples for the best taste.

WAFFLES

Basic Waffle Hints

Here are a few of my rules of thumb for waffle-making:

- *When you buy a waffle iron, read the directions carefully, and then follow them. Most directions will tell you to grease the iron the first time you use it and then wipe clean. Be sure to follow this. There are also irons available that are coated so that you don't have to grease them at all.*
- *Each time you finish using the iron, merely wipe it with a towel and put it away for next time.*
- *Never fill the iron completely with batter. Always fill it one-half to two-thirds full.*
- *Once you have made a dozen waffles, you will understand what I mean when I say that you will know when to lift the waffle iron cover (when the waffle is ready) just by touch. If you lift the lid and it sticks, or resists and doesn't want to come up, leave it for a few more minutes. When the waffle is ready, the lid will lift easily, without any resistance.*
- *Waffles can be made ahead and reheated in the oven. Make them the night before, cool, wrap well, and refrigerate. In the morning, reheat in the oven and serve piping hot.*
- *You can serve any of your favorite toppings with waffles. You may also mix fruit into the waffle batter—try soft bananas, blueberries, raisins, slivered almonds, cooked cranberries, sesame seeds, shredded coconut, powdered sugar, or almost anything your heart desires.*

Speaking of hearts, you can now buy waffle irons in nontraditional shapes like hearts, triangles, or four-leaf clovers. These make theme breakfasts easy!

89

THE EVERYDAY EXTRAORDINARY WAFFLE

1¾ *cups all-purpose flour*
3 *tablespoons sugar*
1 *tablespoon baking powder*
½ *teaspoon salt*
2 *egg yolks, beaten*
1¾ *cups milk*
¼ *cup melted butter or margarine*
2 *egg whites, stiffly beaten*

Preheat waffle iron.

In a mixing bowl, blend the flour, sugar, baking powder, and salt. In a second bowl, combine the egg yolks, milk, and melted butter. Add to the dry ingredients. Beat until well blended. Carefully fold in the stiffly beaten egg whites, leaving a few fluffs of white visible. *Do not overmix!*

Ladle the necessary amount into the hot waffle iron. When done, serve immediately with maple syrup or fruit and powdered sugar.

Serves 2 to 4

CHOCOLATE WAFFLES

Is this everyone's dream? It was mine, so I put them on the menu.

> 2 *cups cake flour*
> 2 *teaspoons baking powder*
> ½ *teaspoon salt*
> 3 *tablespoons sugar*
> 2 *eggs, separated*
> 1¼ *cups milk*
> 1 *teaspoon vanilla*
> 2 *squares unsweetened chocolate*
> ¼ *cup butter or margarine, melted*
> *Pinch of ground cinnamon*

Preheat the waffle iron.

Combine the flour, baking powder, salt, and sugar. Put into the food processor; add 2 egg yolks, milk, and vanilla. Using the steel blade, mix until well blended, about 30 seconds. Remove and pour into a large mixing bowl.

In the top half of a double boiler, over hot water, melt the chocolate, being careful not to burn it. When melted, whisk into the batter.

Add the melted butter to the batter. Mix well. Beat the 2 egg whites until stiff and gently fold into the batter.

Pour batter into the hot waffle iron. (Remember—never fill the iron more than about two-thirds full.) When done, top with cinnamon and serve immediately.

Serves 2 to 4

Hint: Be sure to use cake flour in this recipe. It will make a big difference in the taste of the waffles!

These may be used either as a main course or dessert. If serving as a main course, garnish with unsweetened whipped cream, crème fraîche, or sour cream sprinkled with cocoa powder and fresh fruit.

YOGURT WAFFLES

3 eggs
2 cups all-purpose flour
1 teaspoon baking soda
½ teaspoon salt
3 teaspoons sugar
2 cups nonfat plain yogurt
¼ cup safflower oil

Preheat waffle iron.

Separate the eggs. Beat the whites until stiff. Set aside.

Sift the flour. Stir in the baking soda, salt, and sugar.

Beat the egg yolks. Add to the flour mixture, mixing well. Beat in the yogurt, mixing until smooth. Fold in the beaten egg whites and the oil.

Ladle into the hot waffle iron and cook until golden. Serve immediately.

Serves 2 to 4

Hint: These waffles have a light, tart taste. Garnish with fresh fruit or plain yogurt that has been blended in the food processor or blender for 10 to 15 seconds. You can also top with maple syrup.

FRENCH TOAST

FRENCH TOAST PRINCESS DI
(Or Di's Royal Toast)

1 slice egg bread, lightly toasted
2 tablespoons cream cheese, softened
4 eggs
½ teaspoon vanilla
  Pinch of ground cinnamon
1 tablespoon sweet butter or margarine

Lightly toast 1 slice of egg bread. When cool, spread with cream cheese.

Beat the eggs. Add the vanilla and cinnamon. Dip the cream-cheese-spread bread into the egg mixture. Let it soak.

Melt ½ tablespoon of the butter in a 6- or 7-inch skillet (preferably Teflon, or spray skillet with a vegetable spray like Pam) over medium heat. Place the bread in the skillet and pour the remainder of the egg mixture on the slice. Let it brown.

Melt remaining butter in another 6- or 7-inch skillet over medium heat. When the bottom of the French toast is brown, flip it into the other pan. Remove when crispy—and that's it. Serve garnished with any fruit you like or with pure maple syrup.

Serves 1

Hint: For a change of pace, top with a couple of slices of crisp bacon or Homemade Orange Marmalade (see page 174).

SCULLY'S FRENCH TOAST

My French toast is quite different from the usual. Try it—you may never again make another type of French toast. This recipe is for one person. Four eggs may seem like a lot for one person but the eggs make it fluff up like a baked pancake. You must use my "two pan" method to make this work.

    4 eggs
    ½ teaspoon vanilla
    ¼ teaspoon ground cinnamon
    1 thick slice of homemade white, egg, or raisin bread
    1 tablespoon sweet butter or margarine
    5 fresh strawberries or 1 banana, sliced

Beat the eggs. Add ¼ teaspoon vanilla and ⅛ teaspoon cinnamon. Mix well and pour into a shallow bowl.

Dip the bread slice in the egg mixture. Do this carefully so you don't tear it. Let the bread soak. Melt butter in two 6- or 7-inch skillets (the Teflon kind is best—or spray a regular pan with a vegetable spray like Pam) and heat over a medium flame. When the butter has melted, take one pan off the heat and reserve. Using a spatula, carefully lift the bread from the egg mixture and place in the hot skillet. Pour the remaining egg mixture over the bread, sprinkle with remaining vanilla and cinnamon, and cook until bottom is brown.

Place the reserved skillet over a medium flame. When the French toast browns on the bottom, simply flip it into the second pan to brown the other side. The French toast will look like a fluffy pancake.

When done, place on a warm platter and garnish with fresh sliced strawberries or sliced bananas. You can also top with butter and maple syrup or sprinkle with powdered sugar.

Serves 1

Hint: If you use maple syrup, warm it before serving. Always use pure maple syrup; it's more expensive but tastes better and is more nutritious.

SUNDAY FRENCH TOAST

4 eggs
¼ cup buttermilk (or nonfat plain yogurt, blended)
    Pinch of salt
1 thick slice bread (sour dough is great)
1 tablespoon sweet butter

Beat the eggs until fluffy. Stir in the buttermilk and salt until well blended (you can do this in the food processor using the steel blade). Dip the bread in the mixture until it is soaked.

Melt ½ tablespoon butter in a 6- or 7-inch skillet (preferably Teflon, or spray a regular skillet with a vegetable spray like Pam). Carefully lift the bread from the egg mixture and place in the hot skillet. Pour the remaining egg mixture over the bread and fry until the bottom is brown. Meanwhile, in another skillet, melt the other ½ tablespoon butter. When the bottom of the French toast is brown, flip it into the second skillet and let it brown on the other side.

Serve immediately.

Serves 1

Hint: Top with plain yogurt.

CREPES

BASIC CREPE BATTER

Making crepes is easy—believe me! It may sound fancy and intimidating, but once you've done it, you'll find that it is really simple to do.

> 3 *eggs, beaten*
> 1 *cup milk*
> 1 *cup presifted all-purpose flour*
> 2 *tablespoons sweet butter, melted*
>   *Pinch of salt*
> ½ *teaspoon sugar*

I mix crepe batter by hand. You can also use a food processor—just remember to mix all the liquid ingredients first, and add the dry a little at a time.

In a mixing bowl, beat the eggs and whisk in the milk. Gradually add the flour, stirring constantly with a wire whisk or fork until the mixture is smooth. Add the butter, salt, and sugar. Whisk until the batter is smooth and the consistency of fresh cream.

Use either a crepe pan or a 6-inch frying pan to make the crepes. However, once you use a pan for crepes, do not clean it. Use only for crepes, over and over again. I usually coat the pan with a vegetable spray like Pam to make sure the crepes don't stick.

Heat the pan and spray with Pam or brush with melted butter. Using a soupspoon or a very small soup ladle, pour one crepe at a time into the pan. Pour in just enough batter to lightly coat the bottom of the pan. If holes develop in the crepe, just lift the pan off the fire and tilt pan to move the batter around until it covers the bottom smoothly. After a while this will come naturally, so don't give up. Let the crepe get nicely brown on the bottom (the first one or two may get overdone, but don't worry—once you get the hang of it they will be just fine). Turn the crepe over once and let it cook another few seconds. The second side will never get as evenly brown as the first. It's not a problem as that side will always be the inside and no one will see the difference.

When done, place the crepe on a warm platter and continue making more crepes.

Makes about 20 crepes

Hint: Crepes freeze beautifully, both unfilled and filled. I prefer to make my fillings fresh, so I freeze only unfilled crepes. When I freeze crepes, I put a piece of waxed paper in between each one as they come off the pan. When done, I put them all in a freezer bag (or wrap them in aluminum foil) and place in the freezer. To use, remove the bag or aluminum foil and defrost the crepes. Make your filling, warm the crepes in a toaster or warming oven for 30 seconds or so (*not* in the microwave—they could turn to stone!), fill, and serve.

Hint: After you fill and roll crepes, place them on the dish with the folded side facing down so they don't unwrap.

WHOLE-WHEAT CREPE BATTER

    2 *eggs*
    1 *cup milk*
    1 *cup whole-wheat flour*
    ⅓ *cup finely ground toasted wheat germ*
    2 *tablespoons sweet butter or margarine, melted*
       Pinch of salt (optional)

In the food processor, using a steel blade, beat the eggs. Add the milk and stir to blend. Gradually add the flour and wheat germ, mixing until smooth. Add the melted butter and, if you like, salt. Mix again.

Prepare the crepes according to the recipe on page 96.

Makes 20 crepes

Hint: Wheat germ is a healthy food that adds nutrition to many dishes. One tablespoon contains 5 mgs. iron, 70 gms. phosphorus, 57 mgs. potassium, and 10 units vitamin A. Whenever you think of it, add some to crepes, cakes, breads, or muffins.

APPLE CREPES

1 *pound Homemade Sausage (see page 128)*
1 *tablespoon sweet butter or margarine*
3 *apples, cored, peeled, and sliced thin*
⅓ *cup raisins*
½ *teaspoon ground cinnamon*
12 *crepes (see Basic Crepe Batter, page 96)*

Cook the sausage as directed on page 128. Chop fine and set aside.

Melt the butter or margarine in a skillet over medium heat and add the sliced apples, raisins, and cinnamon. Simmer for 15 minutes or until the apples are tender. Stir in the chopped sausage.

Spoon filling into the center of each crepe. Do not fill too full or it will fall out of the ends. Roll the crepes, allowing 3 per person.

Serves 4

Hint: Apples are great when combined with cheese. If you like, grate some Monterey Jack or Swiss cheese over the top of the crepes. Place in the toaster oven for a few seconds to melt the cheese. Serve immediately.

RASPBERRY-BANANA CREPES

4 *bananas, peeled and thinly sliced into "coins"*
2 *cups raspberries*
8 *crepes (see Basic Crepe Batter, page 96)*
¾ *cup brown sugar*
  Juice of 1 lemon

Preheat oven to 325°.

In a bowl, gently combine bananas and raspberries. Sprinkle each crepe with brown sugar. Divide fruit evenly onto the 8 crepes. Sprinkle brown sugar then lemon juice over the fruit. Roll. Place crepes in a lightly greased baking dish. Heat in oven for 15 to 20 minutes. Serve warm with whipped cream and shredded almonds.

Serves 4

SWEET CREPES

2 *eggs*
⅓ *cup milk*
⅓ *cup water*
¾ *cup presifted all-purpose flour*
1 *tablespoon sweet butter or margarine, softened*
2 *tablespoons sugar*
1 *teaspoon vanilla*
2 *tablespoons cognac (optional)*

In the food processor, using the steel blade, beat the eggs. Continue beating while you add milk and water. Gradually add flour. When smooth, add remaining ingredients. Beat until very smooth. The batter should be the consistency of fresh cream.

Prepare the crepes according to the directions on page 96. Serve with maple syrup topped with sliced fresh fruit and confectioner's sugar.

Makes 20 crepes

Hint: Unless it is against your religion or bad for your health, use the optional cognac. It gives the crepes a delicious flavor!

BLINTZES

1½ cups small-curd cottage cheese, drained
½ cup cream cheese
¼ cup sugar
1 egg, beaten
1 teaspoon vanilla
½ teaspoon freshly grated lemon or orange rind (optional)
8 crepes (see Sweet Crepes, page 99)
2 tablespoons sweet butter or margarine
2 tablespoons confectioner's sugar
1½ to 2 cups sour cream
2 tablespoons strawberry preserves

Preheat oven to 350°.

In the food processor, using the steel blade, mix the cottage cheese, cream cheese, sugar, egg, vanilla, and rind until well blended. Spoon the filling onto the center of each crepe. Arrange, blintz-style, by folding the four sides up and across the filling like an envelope. Turn over so the folded side is down and place in a glass baking dish greased with the butter. Bake for 15 minutes.

Sprinkle each blintz with confectioner's sugar and garnish with sour cream and/or strawberry preserves. Serve immediately.

Serves 4

BEER-BATTER CREPES

2 *eggs*
2 *egg yolks*
1 *cup beer*
1 *cup presifted all-purpose flour*
1½ *teaspoons Mayonnaise (see page 173)*
1 *tablespoon sweet butter or margarine, melted*
¼ *teaspoon salt*

In the food processor, using the steel blade, beat the eggs and egg yolks. While beating, pour in beer. Gradually add the flour, mixing constantly. Add the mayonnaise, butter or margarine, and salt and keep beating until the mixture is fluffy.

Make crepes as directed on page 96.

Makes 25 to 30 crepes

CAVIAR CREPES

2 *crepes (see Basic Crepe Batter, page 96)*
2 *tablespoons sour cream*
1 *tablespoon caviar*
¼ *cup vodka, if desired*

Place crepes on a serving plate. Spoon 1 tablespoon sour cream and ½ tablespoon caviar into center of each crepe and roll. In a saucepan, over low heat, warm vodka. Light with match to ignite alcohol. Pour over crepes and serve immediately.

Serves 1

CREAMED CHICKEN CREPES

4 *chicken breasts, boned, skinned, and cubed*
2 *tablespoons safflower oil*
2 *egg yolks*
1 *cup half-and-half*
2 *tablespoons butter, melted*
¼ *cup all-purpose flour*
   Salt and pepper, to taste
8 *crepes (see Basic Crepe Batter, page 96)*

Preheat oven to 325°.

In a medium skillet, over medium heat, sauté chicken in safflower oil until light brown. In a saucepan, combine egg yolks, half-and-half, butter, flour, and salt and pepper and cook over low heat, stirring constantly, until thick. Add chicken and cook for 3 more minutes.

Spoon creamed chicken into 8 crepes. Roll and place in a greased baking dish. Bake in the preheated oven for 20 minutes. Serve immediately with fresh fruit.

Serves 4

Hint: You can also make another recipe of plain sauce to spoon over crepes when done.

SAUTÉED BANANA-RASPBERRY CREPES

4 *tablespoons butter*
4 *bananas, peeled and thinly sliced into "coins"*
2 *cups raspberries*
2 *tablespoons granulated sugar*
8 *crepes (see Basic Crepe Batter, page 96)*
¼ *cup rum*
4 *tablespoons confectioner's sugar*

In a 9-inch skillet, over low heat, melt butter. Sauté bananas and raspberries with granulated sugar. Cook for about 3 minutes, turning frequently.

Spread crepes out and fill each with the banana-raspberry mixture. Roll. Arrange in a large skillet. Pour rum over the crepes and cook, over low heat, for about 1 minute. Place 2 crepes on each serving plate. Pour any rum remaining in pan over crepes. Dust with confectioner's sugar and serve immediately.

Serves 4

SPINACH RICOTTA CREPES

1 *tablespoon butter or margarine*
2 *tablespoons finely minced onion*
1 *package frozen chopped spinach, thawed and cooked*
1 *cup ricotta cheese*
2 *eggs*
   Pinch of ground cinnamon
   Pinch of grated nutmeg (optional)
8 *crepes (see Basic Crepe Batter, page 96)*
3 *tablespoons sweet sherry (optional)*

Preheat oven to 350°.

In a skillet, over medium heat, melt the butter or margarine. Add the onions and sauté until soft and transparent, but not brown.

In a food processor, using the steel blade, blend the spinach and ricotta cheese. Add the sautéed onions, eggs, and spices.

Spoon filling into each crepe. Roll and place in a greased glass baking dish. If you are using the sherry, pour it over the crepes.

Bake at 350° for about 15 minutes or until warmed through.

Serves 4

CREPES BENEDICT

½ teaspoon Cajun Spice (see page 172)
8 eggs, poached
10 slices bacon, fried and crumbled
8 crepes (see Basic Crepe Batter, page 96)
1 cup Hollandaise Sauce (see page 168)

Preheat oven to 350°.

Sprinkle Cajun spice on each poached egg. Place 1 poached, seasoned egg and equal portions crumbled bacon in each crepe. Fold over as you would an omelet. Cover with hollandaise sauce and a few more bacon bits. Place in the oven for 3 minutes.

Remove from heat and serve immediately, allowing 2 per person, with Home-fried Potatoes (see page 112) and grilled tomatoes.

Serves 4

Hint: Other Crepe Benedict fillings to be topped with hollandaise sauce:
    chopped sausage and fried egg;
    creamed spinach and scrambled eggs;
    browned chopped ham and scrambled eggs topped with a few pieces of sautéed ham.

Another Hint: Sprinkle 1 teaspoon freshly grated Parmesan cheese on top of each filled crepe.

QUICHES

BASIC QUICHE

1 9-inch unbaked deep-dish, puff-pastry pie shell
2 cups cream or half-and-half
3 whole eggs plus 2 yolks
¼ teaspoon salt
⅛ teaspoon white pepper
  Pinch of grated nutmeg
1½ cups grated Swiss cheese

Preheat oven to 375°.

In a medium saucepan, scald the cream or half-and-half (this will hasten the cooking time). Let cool.

In a bowl, beat together eggs, salt, white pepper, nutmeg, and cream or half-and-half.

In the bottom of the pie shell, sprinkle 1½ cups grated Swiss cheese. Pour the custard mixture over it and bake at 375° for 35 to 40 minutes or until set and the top is just brown. Serve warm.

Serves 4 to 6

Hint: Keep pastry cold in refrigerator until ready to use.

QUICHE FILLINGS

To the basic quiche mixture add:

Mexican Quiche. *Jalapeño Jack cheese (in place of Swiss cheese), 1 tablespoon chopped fresh cilantro, ¼ cup diced onion; top with sour cream and fresh cilantro leaves. Serve with a salad.*

Spinach Quiche. *1 cup chopped fresh spinach, ⅛ teaspoon nutmeg, ¾ cup cream cheese and 1½ cups grated Swiss cheese.*

Broccoli Quiche. *1 cup steamed, chopped broccoli florets.*

Zucchini Quiche. *1 cup sliced zucchini sautéed with ¼ cup diced onion and 1 tablespoon butter.*

Carrot Quiche. *3 carrots, thinly sliced and steamed; a pinch each of ground nutmeg, cinnamon, and cloves.*

Fruit Quiche. *2 cups peeled, sliced apples or peaches, or 2 cups sliced fresh strawberries or bananas sautéed over low heat in 1 tablespoon melted butter or margarine until just soft. (For this recipe, omit pepper and salt from Basic Quiche recipe. Add 2 tablespoons sugar or honey and sprinkle or drip over fruit in bottom of pie crust.)*

MR. JIM'S BLUE CHEESE QUICHE

Jim Mahoney is Beverly Hills's public relations maven who loves blue cheese. If you ask him what he would like for breakfast, you can always be sure that he'll start with, "What has blue cheese in it today?" This is his favorite Scully breakfast!

    1 *9-inch unbaked deep-dish, puff-pastry pie shell*
 1⅓ *cups crumbled blue cheese*
    1 *tablespoon butter or margarine*
    2 *tablespoons finely chopped onion*
    3 *eggs plus 2 yolks*
 1½ *cups half-and-half*
   ⅛ *teaspoon ground white pepper*

Preheat oven to 375°.

Place the blue cheese in the pie shell. In a skillet, over medium heat, melt the butter or margarine. Add the onion and sauté until lightly browned. Sprinkle over the blue cheese.

Mix the eggs, half-and-half, and pepper until blended. Pour into the pie shell.

Place the quiche on a baking sheet in the preheated oven and bake for 45 minutes or until set and top is just brown. When done, cool for about 5 minutes, then cut and serve. It is delicious served with a mixed green salad and Cold Cucumber Soup (see page 117) as an appetizer.

Serves 6

Hint: You may use any fine Roquefort or blue cheese. The quality of the cheese will make a difference in the taste of the quiche.

SCULLY'S QUICHE LORRAINE

When I tired of making quiches and took them off the menu, I found that people really missed them. I kept getting requests, so after a while, I put them back in my repertoire. The ingredients for a quiche are usually in the refrigerator. You can make it the day before and it will still be delicious after reheating. It really is a wonderful breakfast dish.

> 1 *9-inch unbaked deep-dish, puff-pastry pie shell*
> 1½ *cups grated Swiss cheese*
> ¾ *pound bacon, baked and chopped into bite-size pieces, cooked very crisp*
> 1 *tablespoon butter or margarine*
> ½ *cup chopped onion*
> 3 *eggs plus 2 yolks*
>   *Pinch of grated nutmeg*
>   *Pinch of ground white pepper*
> 2 *cups half-and-half*

Preheat oven to 375°.

Place 1½ cups grated Swiss cheese on the bottom of pie shell. Sprinkle bacon on top of the cheese. Melt the butter in a small skillet, over medium heat, and sauté the chopped onion until lightly brown. Place onion on top of bacon. Beat the eggs and yolks until fluffy. Add the nutmeg, white pepper, and the half-and-half. Pour over the bacon, cheese, and onions in pie shell.

Place in preheated oven on a baking sheet. Bake for 45 minutes, or until set and top is just brown. Remove from heat and let cool for 5 to 10 minutes. Cut quiche into quarters and serve with a green salad or a side of steamed asparagus or broccoli.

Serves 6

Hint: If you are having 8 to 12 people over for breakfast, you might want to make individual quiches in 2½-inch pie shells.

Another Hint: This recipe fills a deep-dish pie crust. If you use a regular 9-inch crust, you can make two quiches.

TUNA OR SALMON QUICHE

1 9-inch unbaked deep-dish, puff-pastry pie shell
2 tablespoons butter
1 medium onion, chopped fine
1 garlic clove, peeled and crushed
1 12.5-ounce can tuna fish, packed in water, or 1 15.5-ounce can pink salmon, well drained
⅓ cup finely chopped olives, green or black
    Pinch of white pepper
    Pinch of cayenne (optional)
½ cup grated Swiss, Gruyère, or cheddar cheese
3 eggs plus 2 yolks
½ cup half-and-half or cream

Preheat oven to 375°.

In a skillet, over medium heat, melt the butter or margarine. Sauté the onion and garlic until lightly browned.

Flake the tuna or salmon onto the bottom of the pie shell. Sprinkle olives, white pepper, cayenne, and cheese over top of tuna. Beat together eggs and half-and-half. Pour into pie shell. Place the quiche on a baking sheet and bake in preheated oven for about 45 minutes, or until set and top is just brown. Serve with a salad and steamed vegetable.

Serves 6 to 8

Hint: You can use red salmon instead of pink—it is more expensive, but will provide a richer taste.

POTATOES

EASY BOILED POTATOES

12 small red-skinned potatoes
   Butter
¼ cup chopped fresh parsley
½ teaspoon ground nutmeg
   White pepper, to taste

Put the potatoes in a pot and cover with water. Boil for 15 minutes or until done (test with a fork). Drain. Brush with butter, sprinkle with parsley, nutmeg, and white pepper. Serve immediately.

Serves 6

MASHED POTATOES

12 potatoes, peeled and diced
 4 tablespoons butter
½ cup half-and-half
   Salt and pepper, to taste
   Pinch of grated nutmeg

Steam the potatoes. When done, place in food processor bowl. Add butter, half-and-half, and salt and pepper to taste. Blend, using the steel blade, until fluffy. Do not overbeat or potatoes will get starchy. Sprinkle with a pinch of nutmeg.

Serves 6

Hint: Serve immediately with melted butter or Easy Gravy (see page 166).

POTATO SOUFFLÉ

    3 *pounds baking potatoes, unpeeled, cut into chunks*
   ¼ *teaspoon freshly ground black pepper*
    1 *teaspoon salt*
    2 *egg yolks, beaten*
   ¼ *cup sweet butter, softened*
½ to 1 *cup hot milk*
    2 *egg whites*
    1 *tablespoon chopped fresh parsley*
    2 *tablespoons melted butter*

Preheat oven to 375°.

In a large saucepan, boil the unpeeled potatoes for about 30 minutes or until done. Let cool and peel. Using the food processor with the steel blade, blend until smooth. Add the pepper, salt, egg yolks, butter, and milk and blend until the potatoes are smooth and creamy.

Beat the egg whites until stiff. Remove the potatoes from the food processor and gently fold in the egg whites and parsley.

Grease a 2-quart soufflé dish. Put the potatoes into the dish and pour melted butter on top. Bake for about 30 minutes or until the top is light brown. Serve with scrambled eggs or any omelet.

Serves 6

HASHED BROWN POTATOES

    4 *tablespoons butter*
6 to 8 *baking potatoes, peeled and shredded*
        Salt, to taste
        Pepper, to taste

Melt the butter in a large skillet, over medium heat. Add the shredded potatoes, salt, and pepper. Cook, over medium heat, for approximately 15 to 20 minutes or until bottom is well browned. Turn and brown other side.

Serves 6 to 8

Hint: Add diced onions, if desired.

FRIED SWEET POTATOES

4 *large sweet potatoes, peeled and sliced*
4 *tablespoons butter*
  Pinch of grated nutmeg
  Pinch of ground cinnamon
1 *tablespoon chopped fresh parsley (optional)*

Sauté potatoes in butter over low heat until tender, about 15 to 20 minutes, making sure butter doesn't burn. When done, season with nutmeg and cinnamon and sprinkle with chopped fresh parsley, if desired.

Serves 8

Hint: Serve with pure maple syrup and marshmallows on top, heated under broiler until marshmallows are melted. Add more cinnamon if desired.

Another Hint: This is a good dish for a late supper.

HOME-FRIED POTATOES

3 *tablespoons safflower oil*
6 *large baking potatoes, peeled and sliced*
½ *teaspoon salt*
¼ *teaspoon freshly ground pepper*
  Pinch of paprika

In a heavy skillet, over high heat, heat the oil until it is very hot. Lower the flame to medium. Add the potatoes—try to keep as close to one layer as possible. Sprinkle with salt, pepper, and paprika. Cover and cook for about 15 minutes, checking every so often to make sure the potatoes are not burning. You will want the bottom crusty.

Once that occurs, turn the potatoes over. Do this *only once*; this will prevent breaking and keep them from getting soggy.

When the potatoes are done, remove from the pan and drain on paper towels. Serve immediately.

Serves 4

Hint: When peeling potatoes, keep them covered with water to which you have added 1 tablespoon of flour. This will keep them white.

CHEESE POTATOES

> 2 *pounds boiled, peeled potatoes*
> ½ *cup grated Gruyère cheese*
> ½ *cup grated cheddar cheese*
> 1 *cup half-and-half*
> 1 to 2 *tablespoons butter*
> *Salt and pepper, to taste*
> *Pinch of grated nutmeg*

Preheat oven to 350°.

Mash potatoes. Add the cheeses and half-and-half. Put into a greased 1½-quart baking dish, brush top with butter, and bake for 20 to 30 minutes or until the cheese has melted. Sprinkle with salt, pepper, and nutmeg.

Serves 6 to 8

Hint: I love a lot of cheese in this recipe, so for every 4 cups of mashed potatoes I use ½ cup of each cheese. Try making it a couple of times and see how much of each ingredient you prefer. You should make this according to your own taste.

ZINGY POTATOES

      4 tablespoons olive oil
      4 medium potatoes, sliced
      1 medium onion, sliced
      1 clove garlic, mashed
         Pinch of salt
         Pinch of freshly ground black pepper
      ½ cup dry white wine
      ½ cup chicken stock
      ½ teaspoon chopped fresh thyme
      ½ teaspoon chopped fresh marjoram
      1 tablespoon chopped fresh parsley
      1 teaspoon chopped fresh dill

In a large, heavy skillet, heat the oil until very hot. Add the potatoes, onion, garlic, salt and pepper. Let the bottom brown, then turn over. When both sides have browned, add the wine, chicken stock, thyme, and marjoram. Cover and simmer until the potatoes are soft and most of the liquid has been absorbed. Add the parsley and dill and serve immediately with any egg dish.

Serves 4 to 6

Baked Apples (page 21)

Strawberries in Cream (page 22)

An assortment of homemade bre

Eggs Florentine (page 64)

Eggs Indian (page 62)

Mexican Eggs (page 77)

Chocolate Waffle (page 91)

Spinach Ricotta Crepe (page 103)

Chicken Pasta Salad (page 122)

Homemade Sausage (page 128) **and Eggs**

An assortment of smoked fish (page 134)

English Muffins with Homemade Orange Marmalade (page 174)

Enchiladas (page 146)

Smoked Salmon and Caviar Pizza (page 153)

Sautéed Mushrooms on Toast (page 156)

SOUPS

CLASSIC CHICKEN STOCK

4 pounds chicken breast bones

Wash the bones well under cold running water until the water is clear. Put in a large pot, cover with water, and bring to a boil.

Remove the scum from the top. Lower heat and simmer, covered tightly, for 4 hours. Discard the bones and strain stock through an extra-fine sieve (a Japanese one, made of panty hose, is the best). Store, covered, in the refrigerator for 12 hours.

Remove from refrigerator and discard the fat that has formed on the top. You will now have a pure, protein-laden, jellylike chicken stock. It will keep for 4 to 5 days in the refrigerator and may be used for any recipe calling for chicken stock or broth.

Hint: If you want to use this for a soup base, add any fresh vegetables, rice, or pasta and simmer for 30 minutes. It can also be stored in the freezer.

VICHYSSOISE

Ah! The perfect summer late-breakfast/early-brunch soup. It is refreshing, yet filling. And it is so pretty when served in either brightly colored or black soup bowls—both set off the white soup beautifully.

> ¼ *cup butter*
> 8 *medium leeks, chopped (white parts only)*
> 2½ *cups chicken stock*
> 2 *medium potatoes, peeled and chopped*
> 2 *tablespoons chopped fresh chives*
> 1 *tablespoon chopped fresh parsley*
> *Salt and pepper to taste*
> 1 *cup half-and-half*

Melt the butter in a medium saucepan, over medium heat. Stir in the chopped leeks. Sauté until they are pale and golden, about 8 to 10 minutes. Don't let them brown. Add the stock, potatoes, 1 tablespoon chopped chives, and parsley. Season with salt and pepper and simmer, gently, for about 30 minutes. Remove from heat and run through a sieve or blend in the food processor. Cover and let cool.

When cool, gradually add the half-and-half. Taste for additional seasoning. Refrigerate for at least 2 hours.

To serve, spoon the soup into individual bowls and garnish with the remaining chives.

Serves 4 to 6

Hint: Wash leeks well. Dirt always hides under the leaves, so to be sure you are getting it all, remove the leaves one by one and wash under cold running water. Hidden dirt can really mess up a great soup.

COLD CURRY SOUP

> 4 *cups chicken stock*
> 1 *teaspoon curry powder*
> 2 *tablespoons flour*
> 1 *teaspoon butter or margarine*
> ½ *cup half-and-half*
> 1 *apple, peeled, cored, and chopped*
> ¼ *cup chopped fresh cilantro*

In a medium saucepan, over low heat, blend the chicken stock, curry powder, flour, and butter. Cook over a low flame for about 15 minutes. Whisk in the half-and-half. Remove from heat and let cool. Cover and refrigerate at least 1 hour.

Serve with chopped apple and cilantro as garnish.

Serves 4

Hint: Many people don't like the distinctive taste of cilantro. For those of you in this category, don't dismiss this recipe. Garnish with chopped chives or parsley instead, or try sliced bananas and almonds for a slightly different taste.

COLD CUCUMBER SOUP

Some people just don't like cucumbers. A friend of mine maintains that a cucumber is best when it is thrown out. But I love cucumbers— raw or cooked. I particularly love this soup on the terrace while I read the paper or by the pool as I catch the sun. My customers order it all year round—even on a cold winter day.

> 3 *medium cucumbers, scraped and seeded (I prefer hot-house cucumbers)*
> 4 *tablespoons butter*
> 1 *small onion, chopped*
> 4 *cups chicken stock*
> *Salt and pepper, to taste*
> 2 *cups milk*
> ½ *lemon, sliced thin*
> 1 *tablespoon finely chopped fresh dill*
> *Sour cream or yogurt to garnish*

Slice the cucumber, leaving about ¼ cup on the side for garnish. Melt the butter in a skillet over low heat. Sauté the onion until wilted. Stir in the cucumber and continue cooking for 5 minutes. Add 2 cups of the stock, salt, and pepper. Simmer for 15 minutes.

Remove from heat. Place the soup into the food processor bowl. Purée, using the steel blade. Add the milk and remaining stock. Cool. Pour into a freezer tray and freeze for about 30 minutes or until the soup is just slightly frozen.

Serve in soup cups, garnished with a slice of lemon and cucumber. Add a sprinkle of fresh dill and a dab of sour cream or yogurt.

Serves 4 to 6

Hint: I occasionally serve cucumber soup in melon bowls. Use cantaloupe or honeydew melons, one-half for each guest. Scoop out the seeds. Pour the cucumber soup into the cavity, garnish as above, and serve. It's so pretty and it makes a truly memorable beginning to a meal.

COLD MUSHROOM SOUP

Most people are used to eating mushroom soup hot. Try it cold—it is a nice change.

> ½ *pound finely chopped mushrooms*
> 1 *tablespoon chopped chives*
> 4 *small white onions, chopped fine*
> 2 *cups chicken stock*
> 1 *tablespoon cornstarch*
> ½ *cup milk*
>   *Salt and pepper, to taste*
> ½ *cup cream*
> 2 *tablespoons chopped fresh parsley, for garnish*

In a small saucepan, over medium heat, simmer the mushrooms, chives, onions, and stock for 10 minutes.

Mix the cornstarch and milk together. Whisk into the soup and cook, stirring constantly until thick, about 5 minutes. Taste and season with salt and pepper. Remove from heat and cool.

When cool, stir in cream. Pour into soup bowls and garnish with chopped fresh parsley.

Serves 4

Hint: When washing mushrooms, don't let them soak in water as they will retain moisture. Brush with a soft vegetable brush under running water. Dry well with paper towels. Cut off the tips of the stems and chop.

GAZPACHO

 1 *medium cucumber, quartered*
 8 *whole ripe tomatoes, peeled, cored, and halved*
 1 *small green pepper, seeded and quartered*
 3 *scallions*
 2 *cloves garlic, peeled*
    Salt and pepper, to taste
¼ *cup olive oil*
¼ *cup fresh lemon juice or white wine vinegar*
 4 *cups water*
    Chopped olives and/or fresh cilantro, for garnish
 4 *slices bread, toasted and cut into croutons*

In the food processor, using the steel blade, chop the vegetables. Make sure that they don't get too mushy. Place in a large bowl, season, and add the liquids. Cover and refrigerate for an hour or until the soup is very cold.

Serve in ice-cold bowls or cups. Sprinkle with chopped olives and/ or cilantro and croutons. Serve with cheese or garlic toast.

Serves 8

Hint: Gazpacho tastes best when it is very cold. For an added touch, I crush some ice in the food processor and then place a little in each soup bowl. Make the gazpacho the day before you plan to serve it— it tastes even better!

SALADS

HEAVENLY POTATO SALAD

2 *pounds small red potatoes, boiled and unpeeled*
3 *slices bacon*
3 *frankfurters or sausages, sliced*
1 *cup chopped onion*
1 *teaspoon flour*
2 *tablespoons sugar*
½ *teaspoon celery salt*
¼ *teaspoon ground black pepper*
⅓ *cup wine vinegar*
⅓ *cup water*
3 *hard-boiled eggs, sliced*
½ *red pepper, chopped*
1 *tablespoon chopped fresh parsley*

Slice the boiled potatoes and set aside.

In a heavy skillet, over medium heat, sauté the bacon and frankfurters or sausage. When crisp, remove from skillet and drain on a paper towel. Add to potatoes. Using the grease in the pan, make the dressing by blending in ½ cup of chopped onion, flour, sugar, celery salt, pepper, vinegar, and water. Cook over a low flame, stirring occasionally with a wooden spoon, until the dressing is thick.

Pour the dressing over the potatoes and frankfurters. Add remaining onion. Toss in the hard-boiled egg slices and red pepper. Sprinkle with parsley and serve with pumpernickel bread.

Serves 6

CURRIED CHOPPED EGG SALAD

6 *hard-boiled eggs*
1 *tablespoon Mayonnaise (see page 173)*
1 *teaspoon curry powder*
   Pinch of white pepper
   Pinch of salt
¼ *cup diced celery*
1 *tablespoon diced scallions*
½ *small dill pickle, diced*
1 *tablespoon chopped fresh parsley*

Shell the hard-boiled eggs. Chop them into small pieces and place in a bowl. Add the remaining ingredients and blend together. Cover and place in the refrigerator for about 2 hours.

Serve on lettuce with mayonnaise and homemade bread.

You can also use just the yolks of the hard-boiled eggs, leaving the whites halved to fill with the egg salad. Dot the top of each stuffed egg with a drop of Horseradish Sauce (see page 167) or mustard. A sprinkle of paprika or a slice of olive on top completes this delicious stuffed egg.

Serves 4

WHITE BEANS AND TUNA

4 *cups cooked cannellini beans*
2 *6.5-ounce cans white tuna packed in water, drained*
1 *medium onion, chopped*
¼ *cup Vinaigrette Dressing (see page 162) plus 1 table-*
   spoon olive oil

Combine all ingredients and chill for 2 hours. Serve cold on a bed of Belgian endive.

Serves 4 to 6

Hint: Make this the night before. It will give you more time in the morning and it will taste better.

CHICKEN PASTA SALAD

> 1 *16-ounce package corkscrew pasta*
> 4 *chicken breasts, cooked, skinned, and boned*
> 1 *small jar pimentos*
> ½ *cup diced green pepper*
> ½ *cup diced or sliced black olives*
> 1 *small jar artichoke hearts, quartered*
> ½ *cup Fresh Basil Dressing (see page 163)*
> 1 *tablespoon grated Parmesan cheese*
> *Fresh basil leaves, for garnish*

Cook the pasta al dente. Drain and set aside to cool. Slice the chicken into fine, bite-size pieces. Toss the chicken, pimentos, green pepper, olives, and artichoke hearts into the cold pasta. Serve with basil dressing and Parmesan cheese on top. Add some fresh basil leaves as garnish.

Serves 4

Hint: In place of basil dressing, use ½ cup Homemade Mayonnaise (see page 173) into which you have mixed ½ teaspoon curry powder.

MORNING CUCUMBER SALAD

> 1 *cucumber, peeled and sliced*
> 1½ *teaspoons salt*
> 2 *cups nonfat plain yogurt*
> 1 *clove garlic, crushed*
> ½ *teaspoon chopped fresh dill*
> 1 *tablespoon olive oil*
> 2 *tablespoons chopped scallions*
> 1 *tablespoon white wine vinegar*
> 1 *tablespoon chopped fresh mint*
> 8 to 10 *whole fresh mint leaves, for garnish*

Place the cucumber in a large mixing bowl. Add salt and mix. Cover and refrigerate for 1 hour. Drain and set aside.

Combine yogurt with the garlic, dill, oil, scallions, vinegar, and chopped mint. Add the cucumber. Stir to blend. Cover and refrigerate or serve immediately. When ready to serve, garnish with whole mint leaves.

Serves 6

TUNA SALAD

An old favorite, with a new twist.

> 1 *medium onion, diced*
> 1 *small cucumber, peeled and diced*
> ¼ *pound mushrooms, diced*
> 2 *carrots, shredded*
> 2 *hard-boiled eggs, diced*
> ½ *pound fresh spinach, washed well, trimmed, and chopped*
> 2 *stalks celery, diced*
> 1 *head broccoli, steamed and chopped*
> 1 *small zucchini, sliced*
> 1 *tomato, chopped*
> 4 *6.5-ounce cans white albacore tuna packed in water, drained*
> ½ *cup Vinaigrette Dressing (see page 162)*

Combine all ingredients and toss with vinaigrette dressing. Chill, covered. When ready to serve, place the chilled salad on a bed of lettuce leaves. Serve with crackers.

Serves 4

Hint: This is the best kind of last-minute late breakfast dish because it is simple to prepare. You can make your tuna salad in 15 minutes flat. Eggs should be on hand for a simple sweet omelet, then brew the coffee and serve with a smile.

ANCHOVY SALAD

1   *2-ounce can anchovies*
2   *small tomatoes, peeled and diced*
1   *small onion, diced*
      Ground pepper, to taste
1   *tablespoon chopped fresh parsley*

Drain anchovies and reserve the oil. Dice the fillets. Toss together with the tomatoes, onion, and ground pepper. When well blended, stir in 2 teaspoons anchovy oil.

Sprinkle with parsley and serve on a lettuce leaf with freshly baked bread on the side.

To serve additional people, add ½ small onion, 1 small tomato, and 3 to 4 fillets per person.

Serves 2

Hint: Use an excellent imported flat anchovy fillet—it will make a definite difference in the taste.

MEATS

BACON

I'm addicted to bacon! I just love its taste and how it combines with other foods. It wakes up tired old eggs; it virtually sings lying next to tomatoes in a sandwich; it is fabulous with beans or lentils in soup.

Bacon is best when bought at the butcher's freshly sliced. Ask for the leanest piece! You can also use double-smoked bacon (talk about great flavor!), Irish bacon, or Canadian bacon (which is already cooked and tastes and acts more like ham).

Cooking Bacon

Allow 2 slices per person.

Preheat oven to 350°.

Spread the bacon slices in a baking pan. Bake in preheated oven for 15 minutes, or until crisp. As the bacon cooks, pour off all excess grease.

Remove from oven and drain on paper towels. Serve immediately.

If you need to reheat bacon, put it on a paper egg carton (to absorb any extra grease) and place in the microwave oven for 1 minute.

Canadian bacon may be cooked in the same manner, but it requires only 7 to 10 minutes in the oven.

You can also fry bacon in a skillet, but I much prefer it baked. It seems to retain its flavor without being greasy.

BREAKFAST HAM

1 *center cut ham steak, ½ inch thick*
¼ *cup grated Swiss cheese*
¼ *cup grated cheddar cheese*
1 *slice fresh pineapple, cored and peeled*

Preheat broiler.

Trim fat from ham steak. Cover with cheese and place pineapple ring on top. Glaze under broiler until cheese is melted and pineapple is brown. Serve immediately with mustard and cold asparagus.

Serves 1

CHICKEN À LA KING (or Queen)

2½ *cups White Sauce (see page 171)*
¼ *cup chopped pimentos*
½ *cup chopped cooked green peppers*
1 *cup sliced cooked mushrooms*
4 *cooked chicken breasts, cubed*
1 *chicken bouillon cube*
4 *slices toast*
   Pinch of paprika
¼ *cup chopped black olives (optional)*

In a medium saucepan over low heat, combine the white sauce, pimentos, green peppers, mushrooms, chicken, and bouillon cube. Simmer gently until the cube has melted. Stir to blend. Serve immediately on toast. Sprinkle with paprika and garnish with chopped black olives.

Serves 4

Hint: You can also serve this in puff pastry. If you don't have time to make the pastry, you can use frozen pastry shells. Bake them while you make the creamed chicken and keep warm. When the chicken is done, put one puff pastry on each serving dish, spoon the Chicken à la King over it, and serve garnished with olives.

CREAMED CHIPPED CORNED BEEF

2 *cups White Sauce (see page 171)*
1 *pound cooked corned beef, shredded*
1 *small dill pickle, chopped fine*
1 *teaspoon pickle juice*
8 *slices rye toast*
4 *poached eggs (see page 58)*

Make the white sauce, omitting the sherry. Stir in the shredded corned beef. Add the pickle and juice. Divide equally over rye toast. Top each serving with a poached egg. Serve immediately.

Serves 4

Hint: Whenever you make a corned beef sandwich, or if you order one at a delicatessen where they give you enough corned beef on one sandwich to feed a hungry family, save the extra. Refrigerate or freeze it. When you want to make this recipe, put the corned beef in the food processor and chop, using the pulsating tab, or chop by hand.

CHICKEN LIVERS

2 *tablespoons butter or margarine*
12 *chicken livers*
3 *tablespoons flour*
2 *garlic cloves, chopped*
  Salt and pepper, to taste
3 *tablespoons chopped fresh parsley*
2 *tablespoons dry sherry*
½ *cup unsalted chicken stock*

Melt the butter in a heavy skillet, over medium heat. Dredge the chicken livers in flour. Sauté for about 8 minutes or until medium done. Add the garlic, salt, pepper, and parsley. Sauté for another minute. Stir in the sherry and stock. Continue cooking for 2 minutes.

Serve immediately with scrambled eggs and toast.

Serves 4

Hint: Use only fresh livers—never frozen.

HOMEMADE SAUSAGE

1 pound finely ground veal
1 pound finely ground lean top sirloin
1 pound finely ground lean pork
1 tablespoon crushed or powdered fennel seeds
Salt and pepper, to taste

Have the butcher grind the veal, sirloin, and pork at least twice so that it is very fine.

Mix the meat with the seasonings and blend well. Form into 12 patties. Cover and refrigerate overnight.

In the morning, fry the patties until *just* cooked. Don't overcook or they will be dry. Serve 2 per person with eggs, any style, grilled tomato, and Home-fried Potatoes (see page 112).

This sausage is much lower in fat than what you buy ready made. It is full of protein and tastes terrific.

Makes 12 sausage patties

Hint: Crush fennel seeds with a mortar and pestle or buy powdered.

CHICKEN LIVER PÂTÉ

3 tablespoons sweet butter or margarine
1 pound chicken livers
1 large clove garlic, peeled and chopped
¼ cup finely diced onion
½ cup blue cheese
1 cup cream cheese
2 tablespoons sherry
1 tablespoon brandy
Cornichons, for garnish
Fresh toast or crackers

In a heavy skillet, over medium heat, melt the butter or margarine. Sauté the chicken livers, garlic, and onion for 15 minutes. Remove from heat and cool. In the food processor, using the steel blade, blend the liver mixture, blue cheese, cream cheese, sherry, and brandy for about 3 minutes or until very fine. Pour into a greased porcelain mold or soufflé dish. Cover and refrigerate for at least 2 hours.

To serve: Unmold the pâté. Slice and garnish with cornichons and toast or crackers.

This pâté is a delicious treat and easy to make. Prepare ahead of time and it will be one less thing you have to worry about getting ready in the morning.

Serves 8

Hint: I always keep pâté covered with plastic wrap to ensure its freshness.

IRISH STEW

This is not a dish for a 9 A.M. breakfast, but it is perfect for a late noon breakfast on a cold, wintry Sunday, when the winds are blowing and the fireplace is barely keeping your toes warm. Serve with scrambled eggs, homemade Irish Soda Bread, and Irish Coffee (see pages 28 and 196).

> 4 *pounds lean lamb, cut into cubes*
> *Water or chicken stock*
> 3 *medium whole onions*
> 10 *carrots, sliced*
> 16 *small round white potatoes*
> *Pinch of white pepper*
> 1 *sprig fresh rosemary*
> 2 *tablespoons chopped fresh parsley*

Place the lamb in a large pot. Cover with water or fresh chicken stock. Add the onions, carrots, potatoes, pepper, rosemary, and parsley. Bring to a boil. Cover and simmer, on a low flame, for about 2 hours or until the meat is tender to the touch. If you want to thicken the gravy, add a roux made with equal parts butter and flour—but Irish stew should not be thick. For added flavor you can add more parsley and white pepper to the pot.

Serves 8

Hint: Serve with warm Guinness.

SCULLY'S SPECIAL CORNED BEEF HASH

Carol Burnett calls it the best in the world. I don't know if it is, but it is certainly the best I can make. It's also the most popular item on Scully's menu.

> 2 *pounds corned beef, before cooking*
> 1 *small dill pickle*
> ½ *cup sliced carrots*
> 1 *pound small red potatoes, boiled and sliced*
> 1 *cup shredded boiled cabbage*
> 1 *good pinch of white pepper*
> 4 *eggs*
> 2 *tomatoes, sliced, for garnish*
> 1 *dill pickle, for garnish*
> 1 *cup shredded cheddar cheese, for garnish*

In a heavy saucepan over medium heat, cook the corned beef, covered, in water to cover until tender, about 3½ hours. When cooked, trim off all fat, which should leave you with about 1 pound of corned beef.

In the food processor, using the steel blade, purée the pickle. Set aside. Remove the serrated blade and install the slicing blade. Slice the corned beef and mix with carrots, potatoes, cabbage, and pickle. Add the white pepper. You can add a little salt if you wish, but corned beef is often already salty.

Grease a 6- or 8-inch sauté pan with butter. Put the hash in, press down to flatten, and cook over medium heat until it is crisp.

When hash is just about done, poach the eggs (see page 58). Place an egg on top of each serving of hash. Garnish with tomatoes, pickle, and the shredded cheese.

Serves 4

Hint: Serve only to your friends—it's too good for your enemies.

PORK STEW CHILE VERDE

For a late winter breakfast/early lunch.

> 2 *pounds lean pork, cubed*
> 2 *onions, peeled and quartered*
> 2 *tablespoons butter or margarine*
> 4 *cups chicken stock (or to cover)*
> 2 *tomatoes, chopped*
> ½ *cup canned pinto beans*
> 1 *tablespoon chopped jalapeño pepper*
> 1 *16-ounce can ortega chilies*
> *Pinch of Cajun Spice (optional; see page 172)*
> *Pinch of salt and pepper*
> 1 *bunch fresh cilantro, chopped, for garnish*
> 1 *pint sour cream, for garnish*
> *Corn or flour tortillas*

Place the pork in a medium saucepan with the onion. Sauté in 2 tablespoons butter until brown. Add chicken stock and cook for 1 hour or until tender. Add tomatoes, pinto beans, pepper, and chilies and cook for 30 minutes or until all the ingredients have blended into a stew. Season with Cajun spice, if you wish, and salt and pepper. Garnish each serving with 1 tablespoon each of cilantro and sour cream.

Serve with corn or flour tortillas and Mexican beer.

Serves 6

Hint: Make this the day before as it will taste better the next day. Warm it up slowly and, if you need to, thicken with a white roux made of equal parts flour and melted butter, or with a brown roux, made by burning the butter before mixing with flour.

COLD STEAK TARTAR

1½ *pounds finely ground extra-lean beef*
4 *egg yolks*
2 *tablespoons chopped fresh parsley*
2 *tablespoons capers*
1 *tablespoon prepared mustard*
2 *tablespoons finely chopped onion*
4 *dashes of Worcestershire sauce*
  Dash of A-1 steak sauce
6 *pinches of Maggi seasoning*
  Pinch of garlic powder
  Juice of ½ lemon
  Salt to taste
  Pinch of ground black pepper
6 *large anchovy fillets, mashed (optional)*

Garnish

2 *tablespoons chopped fresh parsley*
2 *tablespoons capers*
2 *tablespoons chopped onions*
  Rye-bread rounds
  Crackers or romaine lettuce leaves

Blend the meat and egg yolks together, using a wooden spoon. Add remaining ingredients. Stir until well mixed.

Place in the refrigerator, covered, for at least 1 hour. When ready to serve, form into a large mound on a serving platter. Garnish with the parsley, capers, and onions, each in a separate pile on top of the mound. Surround with rye bread (cut into pretty shapes with a cookie cutter) and/or crackers or romaine lettuce leaves.

Serve with Bloody Marys, sangria, or ice-cold aquavit, and fresh lemon or lime slices.

Serves 6

Hint: You can also make salmon tartar. Use 1½ pounds lightly poached salmon in place of the beef.

FISH

PICKLED HERRING

Herring makes a great side dish for any breakfast—and it's easy to prepare. Just buy it, place it on a serving platter, and garnish with sliced onion and sliced tomatoes.

It is helpful to know the different types of herring available so that you may choose the one that most appeals to your taste. There are more than three kinds of herring, but the ones I use are the most popular and the most readily available. If you are a herring fan, ask to taste the various kinds of herring at your local delicatessen. This will help you delight your guests with new types at your next breakfast get-together. I love to serve a new kind of herring as a side dish with scrambled eggs and watch everyone grin in delight!

The taste actually depends on how the herring was cured. Some are very salty; some, oily; others, sweet; and still others can be quite sour. Of the different kinds of pickled herrings, I recommend the following:

Herring in sour cream: Pickled with onions and sour cream added. It is simply delicious! This is a favorite of my friend Dave Tebet, who orders it every time he comes into Scully's. He's never asked but if he did, I would tell him that I buy mine in the local supermarket, just like everyone else.

Schmaltz herring: Pickled in vinegar and spices. It tastes great with sliced raw onions and tomatoes.

Matjas herring: Pickled in wine. It is my favorite.

Hint: Since herring has such a distinctive taste, a little goes a long way. Serve just one or two pieces as a side dish.

SMOKED FISH

I suggest that you purchase smoked fish from your local fish market rather than those plastic-wrapped from the supermarket. You will be getting a fresher, higher quality fish.

Buy any smoked fish—trout, whitefish, sturgeon, etc.—and bone it (unless you can buy a smoked fillet). Place the fish on a small platter and slice it. Surround slices with ½ cup of sour cream into which you have mixed 1 tablespoon grated fresh horseradish; a sliced red onion, sprigs of parsley, and a lemon sliced into wedges. Sprinkle with freshly ground pepper.

On another platter, place pieces of rye toast and/or thinly sliced pumpernickel bread and a small container of Dijon mustard.

For added luxury, serve with fish knives and forks and hot towels. (Put a dab of perfume on the towels to help eliminate the fish smell.) If you happen to have fish plates, this is the perfect time to use them.

Hint: For a change of pace, serve smoked fish with slices of peeled green apple. The combined flavors of smoked fish and fresh fruit will delight everyone's palate!

SMOKED SALMON

There are a number of salmon choices. You can buy Nova Scotia smoked salmon, Norwegian smoked salmon, Scotch smoked salmon, or American smoked salmon.

Scotch Salmon: The most expensive smoked salmon. It is heavily smoked (dry-cured as opposed to being kept in brine) and is lightly salted. A lovely pink color, it is sliced very thin and frequently served with dill and lemon.

Norwegian Salmon: A fatty smoked fish with more salt than Scotch salmon but less than Nova Scotia. My fish man calls this fish "schmaltzy."

Nova Scotia Salmon: A subtly flavored salmon that is best when sliced more thickly than the others. This is my favorite smoked salmon to use with bagels and cream cheese.

Lox: The saltiest, fattiest, and generally the cheapest. Usually associated with bagels and cream cheese.

Gravlax: This salmon is pressed with dill, salt, sugar, and aquavit until well cured. It is a cocktail party favorite (along with the Scotch salmon), served with a mustard-dill dressing. It is not usually served with bagels or cream cheese.

CAJUN CRAB CAKES

> 1 *pound cooked crab meat*
> 2 *cups mashed potatoes*
> 1 *tablespoon melted butter or margarine*
> 1 *teaspoon Cajun Spice (see page 172)*
> ¼ *cup fresh bread crumbs*
> 2 *egg yolks, beaten*
> ¼ *cup milk*
> 1 *tablespoon butter or margarine*

Mix together the crab meat, mashed potatoes, melted butter or margarine, and Cajun spice until well blended. Form into 8 patties.

Place bread crumbs on a plate. In a small bowl, beat the eggs. Place the milk in another dish. Dip each crab cake into milk, then into egg, and then into bread crumbs. Coat twice.

Melt 1 tablespoon butter or margarine in a skillet over medium heat. Fry the crab cakes until brown on both sides.

I serve these with my Tomato Sauce (see page 170) to which I add ½ teaspoon Cajun spice. If you love tomatoes, grill some slices and serve on top of each crab cake.

Serves 4

Hint: To make this a more traditional late-breakfast dish, poach 1 egg per person and put on top of each crab cake.

CAJUN FISH

1 fish fillet, skinned and boned
1 recipe Cajun Spice (see page 172)
Approximately 1½ cups vegetable oil

Pat fish dry with paper towel. Coat both sides completely with Cajun spice.

Heat an iron skillet. *Do not grease!* (I know your mother told you never to do this, but now that you are grown, you can stop listening to her and do as *I* say.) Heat the pan until it is very, very hot. Then—and only then—pour in ¼ inch of oil. If the pan is hot enough, the oil will not splatter.

When the oil is hot, carefully place the fish in the pan. Cook until black; turn and blacken the other side. Both sides must be black—not brown, but black.

When fish is charcoaled, remove and drain on paper towels. Top with butter and chopped parsley. Serve immediately. To make more servings, simply repeat.

Serves 1

Hint: Serve with boiled potatoes in their skins and some sour cream. If your friends really like to burn, serve some Cajun spice on the side so they can add it to the fish and potatoes. If it's too hot, they'll only have themselves to blame. And besides, they'll remember you forever!

Another Hint: Cajun Fish is not the only thing you can make with this recipe—Cajun just-about-anything is more like it! You can cook steak, chicken, or shrimp in the same manner. I serve Cajun Shrimp with Custard Wild Rice Pudding (see page 150).

FISH CAKES

1 *pound fresh codfish or 1 15.5-ounce can red salmon*
1½ *cups milk*
4 *small red potatoes, peeled*
  Pinch of salt and pepper
  Pinch of paprika
½ *teaspoon butter, melted*
1 *tablespoon finely chopped onion*
1 *teaspoon finely chopped fresh parsley*
¼ *cup fresh bread crumbs*
2 *eggs, beaten*
2 *tablespoons butter or margarine*

If you are using cod: Bone, skin (or ask the fishmonger to do it), and poach gently in ½ cup milk until the fish flakes easily, about 5 to 7 minutes.

If you are using canned salmon: Remove the skin and bones.

Boil the potatoes in 1 cup of milk for about 20 minutes until soft. Remove from heat and mash with the milk.

Mix the fish and potatoes together and season with salt, pepper, paprika, and butter. Add the onion and parsley. Blend together until it looks like a lumpy mashed potato.

Pour the bread crumbs onto a plate. Beat the eggs in a small bowl.

Mold the fish mixture into four cakes, about 1 inch thick and 3 inches across. Alternately dip into the egg and bread crumbs until each cake is thoroughly coated with crumbs. Shake off excess.

Melt the butter or margarine in a heavy skillet, over medium heat. Add the cakes and cook for about 3 to 5 minutes or until both sides are brown.

Serve with Tomato Sauce (see page 170).

Serves 4

Hint: Fish cakes are terrific with a poached egg on top. Spoon the tomato sauce over the top of the egg.

NOODLE-OYSTER AND CLAM LOAF
WITH CREAMED EGGS

¼ *pound uncooked flat noodles*
¾ *cup milk*
¼ *teaspoon salt*
3 *eggs, beaten*
¼ *pint fresh eastern bluepoint oysters*
¼ *pint fresh cherrystone clams*
2 *tablespoons flour*
2 *tablespoons bread crumbs*
6 *hard-boiled eggs*
2 *cups White Sauce (see page 171)*
   Parsley sprigs (optional)
   Pinch of paprika
4 *pieces toast*

Preheat oven to 350°.

Cook the noodles for about 15 minutes in 10 cups water. Drain completely. Reserve the noodles.

Combine the milk, salt, eggs, oysters, clams, and noodles. Mix thoroughly.

Grease a 1½-quart glass casserole. Dust with flour and bread crumbs. Pour in the mixture. Set the casserole in a pan of hot water. Place in the preheated oven and bake for 45 minutes or until the top is brown.

When done, remove from oven and cool for 5 minutes. Unmold onto a serving platter. Cut into ½-inch slices. Slice the hard-boiled eggs and place a couple of slices on each piece. Cover each with 2 tablespoons white sauce. Garnish with a sprig of parsley and a dash of paprika. Serve immediately with toast on the side.

Serves 4

Hint: To make dusting pans or casseroles easier, keep a new powder puff in your flour canister.

CODFISH SALAD

2 *pounds fresh codfish*
6 *medium boiled potatoes, unpeeled and diced*
3 *medium onions, sliced thin*
¼ *cup chopped fresh parsley*
½ *cup Vinaigrette Dressing (see page 162)*

Put codfish in a large pot and cover with water. Cover and refrigerate for 12 hours.

In the morning, poach the fish in the same water for about 10 minutes or until it flakes easily. When done, drain and cool. When cooled, cut into small pieces.

Toss the fish, potatoes, and onions together. Add the parsley and the vinaigrette. If you like, at this point you can add a teaspoonful of Dijon mustard. Mix to blend and serve with homemade or pita bread.

Serves 4 to 6

Hint: Garnish with chopped fresh dill.

SANDWICHES

LOX AND BAGEL SANDWICH

1 fresh bagel, sliced in half
½ cup cream cheese, softened
4 slices smoked salmon
2 slices sweet onion
4 slices beefsteak tomato
6 capers, drained
   Freshly ground black pepper
2 lemon wedges (optional)

Thickly cover each bagel half with cream cheese. Place 2 slices of smoked salmon on each half. Add a slice of onion, 2 slices of tomato, and 3 capers. Provide freshly ground pepper and a lemon wedge for that extra touch.

There are at least two schools of thought on how you eat a bagel and lox sandwich. Some people put the two halves, with all the fixings, on top of one another and try to eat it that way. Try it, but it defies most mouths, even my big one! I prefer to eat the two halves separately. It is easier on the jaw, and you get to enjoy it longer.

Serves 1

Hint: For true decadence, top it all off with a little spoonful of Beluga caviar.

Another Hint: Smoked salmon is very perishable unless refrigerated. You can keep it well wrapped for at least a week in the refrigerator. It may also be frozen, well wrapped, for up to 3 months.

FINGER SANDWICHES

These are great appetizers for your guests while they wait for a heavier brunch—or serve them alone as a late breakfast.

Cut any bread you prefer—white, pumpernickel, rye, sour dough, or wheat—into very thin slices. Spread the slices with softened butter. Use very thin pieces of any meat or vegetable you have on hand to make sandwiches. For instance, sliced cucumber with sour cream, chopped watercress or dill and cream cheese, sardines with a dash of lemon and sliced tomato, or sardines in tomato sauce with capers, etc. The beauty of finger sandwiches is that you can use whatever you have on hand. If you keep a Perfect Pantry, you will have lots of ingredients on hand.

When you have made several sandwiches, trim the crusts and cut the sandwiches into pieces 1 inch wide—hence, the term "finger" sandwiches. If you are in a humorous mood, you can cut them with your cookie cutters in any shapes you like. And cut many—there's something inviting about tiny sandwiches. You'll see—they never last long!

Hint: These are best when made just before eating. When done, cover with a damp cloth to keep fresh until serving time.

EGG AND BACON SANDWICH

  2 *slices homemade Whole-wheat or Basic White Bread (see pages 26 and 24)*
½ *teaspoon Mayonnaise (see page 173)*
    Dash of A-1 sauce
  2 *slices crisp cooked bacon*
  2 *fried eggs*
    Pinch of white pepper

Spread 1 slice of bread with mayonnaise and A-1 sauce. Place the bacon and eggs on it. Sprinkle white pepper on top. Cover with the other slice of bread. Serve immediately.

Garnish with sliced tomatoes sprinkled with white pepper.

Serves 1

Hint: Make sure the egg is fried so the yolk is not soft. If you use an "over easy" egg, the yolk will run off the sandwich.

REUBEN SANDWICH

   2 *slices New York–style rye bread with caraway seeds*
   2 *teaspoons mustard*
   1 *teaspoon Mayonnaise (see page 173)*
   1 *teaspoon chili sauce*
   3 *slices lean corned beef*
 ¼ *cup sauerkraut, drained*
   2 *slices imported Swiss cheese*
   2 *teaspoons melted butter or margarine*
   2 *tablespoons butter or margarine*

Spread the bread with mustard, mayonnaise, and chili sauce. On one slice of bread, layer the cooked corned beef, sauerkraut, and Swiss cheese. Cover with the other slice of bread. Brush both sides of sandwich with melted butter or margarine.

Melt 2 tablespoons butter or margarine in a skillet over medium heat. Sauté the sandwich on both sides until golden brown and the cheese is melted. Remove from heat. Cut into thirds and serve immediately with mustard and a large kosher dill pickle on the side.

Serves 1

Hint: For that extra touch, beat 3 eggs in a flat dish. Dip both sides of the sandwich into the egg batter. Melt 2 tablespoons butter or margarine in a skillet, over medium heat, and sauté the sandwich until it is golden brown.

MONTE CRISTO SANDWICH

   3 *slices egg bread*
   2 *slices turkey or chicken breast*
   2 *thin slices ham*
   2 *eggs*
   1 *tablespoon butter or margarine*
 ¼ *teaspoon confectioner's sugar*
     Strawberry jam
     Sour cream

Make a triple-decker sandwich. Arrange the turkey slices or chicken breast on one slice of bread. Cover with a second slice of bread on which you place the ham. Cover ham with the last slice of bread.

Place a toothpick in each corner of the sandwich. Beat the eggs and pour into a flat plate. Dip both sides of the sandwich into the egg until well soaked.

In a skillet, over medium heat, melt the butter or margarine. Place the sandwich in the skillet and sauté on both sides. Pour any extra egg over the sandwich while cooking. When the sandwich is golden brown, remove toothpicks, place sandwich on a serving plate, sprinkle with confectioner's sugar and garnish with a dab of strawberry jam and sour cream. Serve immediately.

Serves 1

TUNA MELT

2 *slices rye bread*
1 *6.5-ounce can water-packed white albacore tuna, drained*
2 *tablespoons Mayonnaise (see page 173)*
1 *tablespoon diced onion*
1 *teaspoon capers*
1 *tablespoon diced celery*
   Pinch of cayenne pepper
4 *slices Swiss cheese*
2 *slices green pepper*
2 *thin slices onion*
   Dill pickles and Horseradish Sauce (see page 167) for garnish

Toast the rye bread until it is slightly brown. Set aside. Mix the tuna with the mayonnaise, onion, capers, celery, and a pinch of cayenne. Blend well.

Place 1 slice of Swiss cheese on each slice of toast. Cover with tuna salad, another slice of cheese, a slice of pepper, and an onion slice. Place the sandwich under the broiler and broil until the cheese is melted over the top of the tuna. Serve with dill pickles and horseradish sauce on the side.

Serves 2

Hint: Serve on thick, double-baked, deli rye bread.

ENGLISH ROQUEFORT SANDWICH

2 *slices sour-dough or egg bread*
   Approximately ½ cup Roquefort or other blue cheese
   Pinch of cayenne pepper
1 *tablespoon slivered almonds*
½ *teaspoon chopped fresh parsley*

Preheat oven to Broil.

Cover each slice of bread with cheese. Sprinkle with cayenne. Place under the broiler until the cheese just begins to melt.

Remove from heat and sprinkle with almonds. Return to broiler until the almonds are light brown. Remove from broiler and sprinkle with the parsley. Serve immediately.

Serves 2

SMOKED STURGEON SANDWICH

Ah! The taste of smoked fish in the morning—what a treat! Sturgeon is an especially delicious smoked fish found in most good delicatessens. It is the king of fish! Once you've tasted it, you may find it hard to go back to smoked salmon.

2 *slices pumpernickel bread*
1 *tablespoon butter or margarine*
4 *slices (about ¼ pound) smoked sturgeon, boned*
8 *thin slices hothouse cucumber*
1 *tablespoon caviar (even salmon roe will taste great!)*
   Dash of fresh lemon juice (optional)

Butter bread. On each slice, place 2 slices of sturgeon, cover with 4 slices cucumber and top with caviar. Squeeze a few drops of lemon on top. Serve as an open-faced sandwich.

Serves 1

Hint: If you're eating alone or with a very close friend, add thinly sliced onions before the cucumber slices.

Another Hint: Ask for center-cut slices of sturgeon—they're the best.

MOTHER'S SANDWICH ITALIANA

1 loaf Italian or French bread
1 clove garlic, halved
1 medium cucumber, peeled and sliced
1 medium tomato, sliced
1 2-ounce can anchovy fillets, drained and mashed
8 Italian or Greek olives, pitted and halved
1 tablespoon olive oil
1 teaspoon wine vinegar

Slice the bread in half, lengthwise. Rub the cut sides with garlic. On the bottom half, arrange slices of cucumber and tomato. Cover with mashed anchovies and olives. Sprinkle with olive oil and vinegar. Cover with the other half of the bread. Cut into individual sandwiches and serve immediately.

Serves 6

MISCELLANEOUS

ENCHILADAS

    4 corn tortillas
    2 cups shredded cheddar and Monterey Jack cheese, mixed
       together
    1 cup enchilada sauce (commercially available)
    8 pitted black olives, diced
 1½ cups shredded lettuce
    8 sprigs cilantro, for garnish (optional)
  ¾ cup Salsa (see page 169)

Preheat oven to 350°.

Heat the tortillas on top of gas burner to soften (watch carefully so
they don't burn). Reserving ¼ cup for garnish, place equal amounts
of the cheese on each tortilla and roll up. Place in a greased baking
dish, smooth side up. Pour the enchilada sauce over all and sprinkle
with diced olives and reserved cheese.

Bake in preheated oven for 25 minutes or until the cheese has melted
and is bubbly. Remove from heat and place carefully on a serving
plate. Top with shredded lettuce, cilantro (this is optional, as it has
a very distinctive taste that you may not like), and fresh salsa.

Serves 2

Refried Beans

If you like, you can serve refried beans with the enchiladas. Cook 1
cup dried pinto beans in water to cover until tender. When done,
mash with a fork. While hot, blend in 2 tablespoons shredded cheese
and 1 tablespoon finely chopped onion. Sauté in a skillet with 1
teaspoon oil until the cheese has melted and the beans are a bit crisp.

CHEESE SOUFFLÉ

Mention the word "soufflé" and even the most experienced cook has been known to hyperventilate. I am here to tell you that making a soufflé is *not* difficult, nor is it time-consuming. You can ready the roux and, at the last minute, add the egg whites and bake. It is so simple to impress your guests!

> ¼ *cup butter*
> ¼ *cup sifted flour*
> ¼ *cup grated Parmesan or imported Swiss cheese*
> 1 *cup milk*
> 3 *egg yolks*
> 6 *egg whites*

Preheat oven to 375°.

In a saucepan, over medium heat, melt the butter. Stir in the flour. Blend into a roux using a wooden spoon. Add the grated cheese and milk. Stir until thick. Add the yolks one at a time and, with a whisk, beat until thick.

Beat egg whites until stiff. Fold into the sauce.

Butter and flour a 6-inch soufflé dish. Pour the mixture into the dish, but do not fill it to more than 1 inch from the top. Place in the oven on the middle shelf. Remove the top shelf so the soufflé has room to rise. The soufflé will rise the entire time it is in the oven and will come up about 1 inch higher than the soufflé dish. Bake for 40 minutes. Once you take the soufflé out of the oven, it will begin to fall, so have all other dishes ready to serve *before* you take it out.

A cheese soufflé makes a wonderful light meal when served with a simple green salad.

Serves 2

Hint: Before beating the egg whites, let them warm to room temperature. This will give them greater volume when beaten.

Another Hint: If your soufflé is a little soft in the center, don't panic— as a matter of fact, I prefer it that way. A dry soufflé is not a perfect one. In the "old days," on the ship, we used the soft center as the sauce for the soufflé.

CARMEN'S BREAD 'N' MILK

Carmen is my older sister. She taught me how to make this when I was six. I never forgot it and I still love it.

1½ *cups milk*
  2 *slices white bread, trimmed of crusts and cut into*
     1-inch squares
     Pinch of grated nutmeg
  1 *teaspoon sugar*

Scald the milk. Add the cut-up bread. Stir in the nutmeg and sugar. Let cool and eat.

Serves 1

Hint: This is a "make-you-feel-better" dish. It's very refreshing, very good for the stomach, and a great breakfast dish for the morning after. When you feel better, have it again, but this time drop a scoop of vanilla ice cream right into the middle.

CHEESE TOAST

  2 *tablespoons butter*
1½ *tablespoons flour*
 ½ *cup milk*
 ½ *cup grated Gruyère cheese*
  3 *tablespoons dry white wine*
  1 *clove garlic, minced*
  1 *egg, beaten*
     Salt and pepper, to taste
     Pinch of grated nutmeg
 12 *slices French bread, cut diagonally*

Preheat oven to Broil.

Melt the butter in a skillet over low heat. Blend in the flour. Gradually add the milk and stir with a wire whisk until it boils. Remove from heat. Cool.

Add cheese, wine, garlic, egg, salt and pepper, and nutmeg. Stir well but do not let it cook.

Toast sliced French bread on one side. Spread the untoasted side with cheese mixture. Broil until lightly browned.

Serves 5 to 6

Hint: Serve fresh grated Parmesan cheese on the side for an even cheesier taste. You may also mix Parmesan with the butter when you melt it.

CHILE RELLENO

6 *eggs, separated*
1 *teaspoon baking powder*
1 *tablespoon flour*
1 *5-ounce can ortega chilies (or 4 whole fresh ones, if you prefer)*
1 *cup cubed Monterey Jack cheese*
1 *tablespoon butter or margarine*
4 *tablespoons Salsa (see page 169)*
4 *tortillas*

Separate the eggs. Beat the yolks until thick. Set aside.

Beat the egg whites. While beating, gradually add the baking powder and flour and continue beating until stiff. Fold the beaten whites into the yolk mixture. Set aside.

Slice the chilies open on one side and stuff with cheese. (Leave the chilies whole, just slice open so you can stuff them.) Dip the chilies, one at a time, into the egg mixture. Melt the butter in a skillet, over medium heat, and let it get very hot. Place the chilies in the skillet and sauté them on both sides. They will look like little omelets—the cheese will melt and the egg batter around the chile will resemble a little pancake.

Allow 2 chilies per person and serve salsa and warm tortillas on the side.

Serves 2

Hint: This is terrific garnished with sour cream, sliced avocados, and chopped onion.

CUSTARD WILD RICE PUDDING

2 *eggs*
1 *cup half-and-half*
¼ *cup heavy cream*
1½ *teaspoons brown sugar*
1 *cup cooked wild rice, loosely packed*
2 *tablespoons peeled and chopped apple*
2 *teaspoons raisins*
Pinch of grated nutmeg
Pinch of ground cinnamon

Preheat oven to 325°.

Beat eggs. Add half-and-half, heavy cream, and brown sugar. Set aside.

Combine the rice, apple, and raisins. Spoon equal amounts into two greased 4-inch soufflé dishes and pour egg and cream mixture on top. Sprinkle with nutmeg and cinnamon. Bake 1 hour in preheated oven. When cool, shake confectioner's sugar on top. Serve warm or cold.

Serves 2

Hint: Serve with Cajun Shrimp (see page 136) or as a lovely, not-too-sweet dessert topped with vanilla ice cream.

EGG-AND-CHEESE CUSTARD

4 *eggs*
1½ *cups milk*
1 *teaspoon salt*
⅛ *teaspoon pepper*
½ *cup grated Swiss cheese*
1 *tablespoon grated cheddar cheese*
1 *cup Tomato Sauce (see page 170)*

Preheat oven to 250°.

Grease a 1½-quart glass baking dish. Beat the eggs. Stir in the milk, seasonings, and cheese. Pour into prepared dish.

Put the dish in a pan of hot water. Place in the oven and bake for 25 to 30 minutes or until the custard is firm. Remove from the oven and let stand on the counter for about 5 minutes. Turn it onto a platter. Cover with tomato sauce and serve immediately.

Serves 4

Hint: Place slices of ham, tomato, or cooked bacon on the bottom of the baking dish before you add the custard.

ESCARGOTS WITH MUSHROOMS

2 *tablespoons sweet butter*
1 *7-ounce can escargots (or 12 escargots)*
5 *fresh mushrooms, sliced thin*
1 *teaspoon chopped shallots*
1 *teaspoon mashed garlic*
4 *tablespoons chopped fresh parsley*
½ *cup chicken stock*
2 *slices white toast*
    Pinch of white pepper
    Squeeze of fresh lemon juice
    Dash of brandy
    Pinch of grated nutmeg

Melt 1 tablespoon butter in a medium skillet over low heat. Sauté the escargots, mushrooms, shallots, and garlic until the shallots are lightly browned and the mushrooms are soft. Add the parsley. Pour in chicken stock and reduce to a thin sauce. Continue cooking, stirring occasionally, until the sauce becomes sticky.

Serve immediately with 2 slices fresh white toast. Add a little pinch of white pepper, a squeeze of lemon juice, a dash of brandy, and a hint of grated nutmeg as you serve.

Serves 1 to 2

Hint: Serve with or on Cheese Toast (see page 148).

PIZZA

Think breakfast—think pizza! Tomato and cheese is a great taste treat for a breakfast or brunch. Or try any of my toppings listed below—you may find that pizza with smoked salmon, cream cheese, and caviar will replace bagels and cream cheese! Making pizza is easy enough to do early in the morning. And besides, I love to try new toppings, new combinations, and new ideas.

Dough for Two Pizzas

1 cup warm water
1 packet dry yeast
1 teaspoon sugar
½ teaspoon salt
2 tablespoons olive oil
3½ cups sifted all-purpose flour
2 tablespoons melted butter

Preheat oven to 375°.

Pour water into a medium bowl. Add yeast and stir until dissolved. Pour into the food-processor bowl. Using the steel blade, blend in the sugar, salt, olive oil, and 2 cups of flour until smooth. When smooth, add the remaining flour and beat until a stiff dough is formed.

Place the dough on a floured cutting board. Knead until soft and pliable. Place in a greased bowl and brush with a little olive oil. Cover with a towel and place in a warm spot for 1 hour or until the dough rises to double its size.

Divide the dough in half. We'll make one pizza and refrigerate the other half of the dough, well wrapped, for later use. Form the dough into a ball and, using a rolling pin, roll out to a 12-inch circle or one large enough to fill your pizza pan. Grease the pan with melted butter and place the dough in it. Brush with olive oil. Spread topping on the pizza dough and bake for 20 to 25 minutes or until the crust around the edge is brown.

Toppings:

○ *Smoked salmon, cream cheese, sour cream, topped with caviar;*

○ *Italian Tomato Sauce with:*
  fresh mushrooms (try exotic ones);
  artichoke hearts;
  chopped chives;
  chopped celery;
  sliced zucchini;
  cooked hamburger;
  slices of any favorite meats;
  2 cups shredded Parmesan or mozzarella cheese;
  1 cup each roasted green and red peppers (you can buy them in a jar or simply roast them in the broiler, peel, and marinate for 1 day in olive oil and chopped fresh basil).

Hint: You can make the dough the night before and refrigerate.

GRILLED TOMATOES

4 large ripe tomatoes
1 tablespoon melted butter
1 clove garlic
1 tablespoon bread crumbs
1 tablespoon grated Parmesan cheese

Preheat oven to Broil.

Wash 4 large, fresh, ripe tomatoes. Cut each in half and brush with melted butter. Mash garlic and sprinkle some on each tomato half. Cover with bread crumbs and grated cheese. Grill in the broiler for about 10 minutes or until top is brown. Serve immediately.

Serves 8

ONION SOUFFLÉ

2 *tablespoons sweet butter or margarine*
2 *tablespoons flour*
¼ *cup milk*
½ *cup heavy cream*
2 *white onions, peeled, chopped fine, and sautéed*
3 *egg yolks*
   Pinch of salt
   Pinch of ground cinnamon
4 *egg whites*

Preheat oven to 325°.

Grease a 7-inch soufflé dish and set aside. In a heavy skillet over low heat, melt the butter or margarine. With a wooden spoon, stir in the flour. When it is well blended, add the milk and cream. Cook until thick and creamy. Add the onions. Simmer for 2 minutes. Remove from heat.

Beat the egg yolks and whisk them into the mixture. Stir well and season with the salt and cinnamon.

Beat the egg whites until stiff. Fold into the onion base. Pour into prepared soufflé dish and bake for about 30 minutes, until soufflé rises and is lightly browned on top. Watch to make sure it rises but does not burn. If it seems ready before (or after) 30 minutes, take it out. But, remember—once you take it out of the oven, you can't put it back in! And please, don't keep opening the door to check the soufflé—this will make it fall.

Serves 4

Hint: Cook the onions for at least 30 minutes on a low flame, until they are brown and sweet tasting. You can do this the night before and store them, covered, in the refrigerator. In the morning you'll be ready to go, and you won't be chopping onions and crying just as your guests are arriving. If the onions were refrigerated, make sure they have been at room temperature for at least 15 minutes.

WELSH RAREBIT

This is from my neck of the woods. Yet you would be surprised at how many Hollywood folk ask for this traditional English dish.

1 *tablespoon butter or margarine*
1 *tablespoon flour*
2 *tablespoons milk*
⅓ *cup beer*
1 *tablespoon Worcestershire sauce*
1 *teaspoon prepared mustard*
  Pinch of salt
  Pinch of pepper
2 *cups grated cheddar cheese*
4 *slices toast*
4 *Grilled Tomato halves (see page 153)*
  Crisp bacon (optional)

Preheat oven to 400°.

In a small pan, over low heat, melt the butter or margarine. Add the flour and stir to blend. Gradually add the milk, beer, Worcestershire sauce, mustard, salt and pepper, stirring constantly until smooth. Add the cheese and keep cooking until the cheese melts and sauce thickens.

Place slices of toast on a baking sheet or in a heatproof casserole and pour equal portions of sauce over each slice. Turn the oven to Broil, and broil the rarebits for 2 to 3 minutes, or until the top gets brown. Watch carefully—you don't want to go to all this trouble just to watch them burn!

When they are done, put two each on a serving plate, garnish with grilled tomatoes and, if desired, bacon, and serve immediately.

Serves 2

Hint: Serve Worcestershire sauce on the side. Be sure to have extra slices of buttered toast ready—people always like to dip more bread in the rarebit.

SAUTÉED MUSHROOMS ON TOAST

This is Ed and Victoria McMahon's favorite dish. Also Baby Katherine's.

12 *medium-size mushrooms*
 1 *tablespoon butter*
   Pinch of salt and white pepper
 1 *tablespoon chopped fresh parsley*
 1 *clove garlic, mashed*
½ *cup Chicken Stock (see page 115)*
 2 *slices toast, crusts removed, cut into 8 triangles*

Wash the mushrooms well and dry with a paper towel. Cut off the tip of the stem and slice in half. In a heavy skillet over low heat, melt the butter or margarine. Add mushrooms, salt, white pepper, parsley, garlic, and chicken stock. Sauté until golden brown.

Place 4 toast triangles on each serving plate. Spoon mushrooms and sauce over toast. Serve immediately.

Serves 2

Hint: This is an easy dish to make for 3 to 4 people. Just double the recipe.

Another Hint: Make it a sinful dish—crisp some bacon and serve as a garnish on top of the mushrooms.

TACOS

Tacos are wonderful for a breakfast party. They are easy to make and a fun treat. I don't know why, but people don't usually make tacos at home, even though they are so simple to prepare.

8   *corn tortillas*
2   *cups sautéed ground beef*
2   *cups chopped onions*
2   *cups chopped olives*
2   *tablespoons chopped fresh cilantro*
2   *cups cooked, shredded chicken*
2   *cups shredded cheddar cheese*
2   *cups shredded Monterey Jack cheese*
2   *cups Salsa (see page 169)*
3   *cups Refried Beans (see page 146)*
    Chicharrones (pork skins baked in the oven until all the
    fat is off), chopped

Have all the ingredients ready in separate small bowls. Heat the tortillas in the oven. When they are soft, bend them in half so they can hold the filling. Serve the empty shells to your guests and let them fill with any or all of the fillings.

Makes 8 tacos

Hint: These are "soft" tacos. If you like yours crispy, you can buy folded tortillas ready-made. If you are having more than four guests, you shouldn't have to worry about deep-frying tacos, so don't hesitate to take this short cut.

TORTILLA CARNE

¼ *cup sweet butter or margarine, or ¼ cup safflower oil*
1 *clove garlic, minced*
1 *small onion, chopped fine*
4 *tomatoes, peeled and chopped*
½ *pound lean ground beef*
  Pinch of salt and pepper
3 *eggs*
1 *tablespoon butter or margarine*
  Corn tortillas

Melt the ¼ cup butter or oil in a skillet, over medium heat, until very hot. Quickly fry the garlic (garlic burns very fast, so be careful!). Lower heat and add the onion. Sauté until soft. Add the tomatoes, meat, salt and pepper, and mix well. Cook for 1 minute. Set aside to cool.

Beat the eggs until light and frothy. Add to the meat mixture.

In another skillet, over medium heat, melt 1 tablespoon butter or margarine. Drop the beef mixture by the tablespoonful onto the skillet. Brown on both sides.

Serve immediately with soft or crisp corn tortillas (to crisp them, merely fry them in butter).

Serves 2

Hint: For added spice, add chopped fresh cilantro or diced jalapeño peppers to the meat before cooking.

Another Hint: To peel tomatoes, drop them into boiling water for about 30 seconds. Take them out of the pot (use tongs) and let cool for about 1 minute. The skin will slip right off.

OATMEAL

Oatmeal is the finest thing I know of for cleaning the arteries of cholesterol. (Ask your doctor if you like!)

½ cup imported oats
1 teaspoon sweet butter
Pinch of ground cinnamon
¾ cup bottled water
1 tablespoon raisins (optional)
1 tablespoon chopped apple (optional)
1 tablespoon chopped nuts (optional)
½ cup half-and-half or milk
1 teaspoon sugar or honey

Place ½ cup oats in a medium saucepan with butter, cinnamon, and bottled water—yes, bottled water; it will make a difference in the taste! Cook over low heat until the oats thicken but are still loose and liquid. Do not overcook, as they become gooey. Stir in the raisins, apple, or nuts, if you like.

Serve in a pretty bowl with half-and-half or milk, or, if you like your oatmeal sweet, add sugar or honey to taste. Try serving with apple or orange juice—it's surprisingly refreshing!

Serves 1

Hint: Remember—the bottled water will make the difference in the great taste of this oatmeal.

Another Hint: Use the finest imported oats you can buy. They're a little more expensive but they're worth it. I use Scott's Natural Oats.

QUESADILLAS

Per person:

> 1 *large flour tortilla*
> ½ *cup grated Monterey Jack cheese*
> 1 *large ortega chili*
> 1 *tablespoon chopped onion*
> 1 *teaspoon melted sweet butter*
> 1 *scallion, chopped*
> 1 *tablespoon sour cream*
> 1 *tomato, chopped*
> ½ *cup shredded lettuce*
> 6 *sprigs fresh cilantro, chopped*
> ¼ *cup grated cheddar cheese*
> ½ *cup hot sauce (homemade or commercial)*

Homemade Hot Sauce:

> 1 *small tomato, chopped*
> ⅛ *cup chopped green pepper*
> ⅛ *cup chopped onion*
> ½ *tablespoon chopped fresh cilantro*
> *Dash of Tabasco sauce, if desired*

Preheat oven to 350°.

If making homemade hot sauce, combine all ingredients and set aside. Place a tortilla in a baking dish. Fill one half of it with cheese, chili, and onion. Fold the tortilla in half so that all the ingredients are inside and brush with melted butter.

Place in the oven for 15 minutes or until the cheese has melted. Remove from heat and top with scallion, sour cream, tomato, lettuce, cilantro, ¼ cup cheddar cheese, and hot sauce.

Serves 1

RACLETTE

A wonderful Swiss cheese called "raclette" is used to make this break-fast dish. It is a favorite of skiers in the Swiss Alps, where it is served as a pick-me-up as they come off the slopes.

½ pound raclette

Preheat oven to Broil.

Place the cheese in an ovenproof dish. Put under the broiler and heat until the top is burned. Don't worry about ruining the cheese—it will be burned on the outside but nice and soft inside.

Remove the dish from the broiler. Serve the cheese just as it is with warm rye bread and cornichons. You can also garnish with sautéed onions and boiled potatoes. To eat, scrape with a knife and place, a bite at a time, on the bread. To quench your thirst, have some kirsch or a dry white wine. Perfecto!

Serves 4

Hint: Don't serve water with this dish—it is not good for your digestive system!

DRESSINGS

SCULLY'S VINAIGRETTE DRESSING

  1 cup safflower oil
  ¼ cup apple-cider vinegar
  ¼ cup fresh mushrooms
  ½ white onion
  1 tablespoon capers
  1 medium dill pickle
  3 hard-boiled eggs
1½ tablespoons dried tarragon
  ½ teaspoon salt (optional—I don't use it, but if you miss
     it, go ahead and use it)

In the food processor or blender, mix all the ingredients. They will form a thick dressing. If it is too thick for your taste, add a little vinegar if you want it sharp or a little water if you like it on the mild side.

This dressing is a favorite at Scully's—my friend Deborah Raffin asks for it so often I sometimes make some extra for her to take home. Do the same for your guests—it is an easy and generous way to give some of your home to them.

Makes 2 cups

Hint: If you really want to make this fantastic, use fresh instead of dried tarragon.

FRESH BASIL DRESSING

This is not cheap to make because basil is expensive, but it is worth it. You simply cannot make a good dressing from dried basil leaves.

    4 cups safflower oil
1½ cups apple-cider vinegar
    4 tablespoons water
    2 eggs
   ½ teaspoon salt
8 to 10 bunches fresh basil, washed and stems removed

Pour the oil into the food processor. Add the vinegar, water, eggs, salt, and the basil leaves. Blend and pour into a small pitcher or bowl.

You can keep this dressing in the refrigerator for about 3 to 4 days. It is wonderful on steamed vegetables, salad, and as a sauce for fish.

Makes 6 cups

Hint: To keep basil leaves fresh, wash well, wrap in paper towels, place in a plastic bag, and refrigerate.

HONEY/LEMON/DILL/GARLIC DRESSING

    1 bunch fresh dill, washed and stalks removed
   10 large cloves garlic, peeled
    1 cup safflower oil or soy oil
   ¼ cup apple-cider or rice vinegar
   ¼ cup honey
     Juice of 2 lemons
   ¼ cup bottled water

Blend the dill and the garlic cloves in your food processor or blender. Add the rest of the ingredients and mix thoroughly until the dill is finely puréed.

Makes 2 cups

Hint: Use this dressing not only on salads, but on any steamed vegetables.

PEANUT DRESSING

1 *cup sesame-seed oil*
¼ *cup unsalted dry-roasted peanuts*
1 *tablespoon soy sauce*
2 *tablespoons honey*
⅓ *cup rice vinegar*
2 *tablespoons brown sugar*

Blend all the ingredients in the food processor. If the dressing is too thick, add a little water to thin it down. This dressing is just the thing to wake up a salad.

Makes 2 cups

Hint: Be sure to use unsalted peanuts—you don't need the extra salt. Besides, the tastes of sugar and salt don't mix well.

SAUCES
AND
CONDIMENTS

SAUCES

CUSTARD SAUCE FOR POACHED FRUIT

> 2 *egg yolks*
> 2 *tablespoons super-fine sugar*
> 1½ *cups milk*
> 2 *tablespoons cornstarch*
> ½ *teaspoon vanilla*

Beat the egg yolks. Stir in sugar and set aside. In the top half of a double boiler, over boiling water, bring the milk to a boil. Pour hot milk, a few drops at a time, into the egg-yolk mixture, stirring constantly until all milk has been added. Pour back into the top of the double boiler, whisk in cornstarch, and cook, stirring constantly until thick. Remove from heat and chill. When cold, stir in the vanilla. Coat each serving plate with custard sauce, place fruit in center, and cover with custard.

Makes 2 cups

Hint: If you want to use this as a custard rather than a sauce, put some fruit in the bottom of a serving dish, pour the custard over it, and chill.

SCULLY'S DEVON CREAM

1 quart sour cream
1 tablespoon brown sugar
1 tablespoon vanilla

Blend all ingredients in your food processor, using the steel blade. Serve immediately or cover tightly and refrigerate. This will keep, refrigerated, until the expiration date on the container of sour cream you use.

Makes 2 cups

SCULLY'S EASY GRAVY

1 teaspoon butter
1 teaspoon flour
1 can beef consommé
Dash of Worcestershire sauce

Melt butter in a small saucepan over medium heat. Stir in flour and let cook for a few minutes. Stir in consommé, add Worcestershire sauce and whisk constantly until thick. Remove from heat and serve immediately. Pour over buttermilk biscuits, mashed potatoes, or poached eggs.

Makes 1½ cups

GREEN SAUCE FOR BLOODY MARYS

½ bunch fresh cilantro, chopped
1 small chili pepper
1 pound green tomatillos
2 thin slices white onion
4 tablespoons water

In the food processor, using the steel blade, purée all ingredients. Cover and refrigerate until ready to use.

Makes enough for 4 Bloody Marys

Hint: This will keep, covered and refrigerated, for 3 days.

EASY HOLLANDAISE

In case you don't have the time to make the more complicated sauce, here's an easy recipe for hollandaise. It won't be the "real" thing, but it will do.

1½ cups White Sauce (see page 171), warmed
3 egg yolks, beaten
3½ tablespoons fresh lemon juice
   A couple of pinches of cayenne pepper

In a small saucepan, over low heat, add the eggs to the *warmed* (not hot) white sauce, beating constantly. When well blended, remove from heat and add lemon juice and cayenne. Stir to mix. Serve immediately. (Use as you would regular hollandaise sauce.)

Makes 1½ cups

Hint: Use this only in an emergency. Otherwise, take the time to make the real thing.

HORSERADISH SAUCE

1 tablespoon sweet butter or margarine
½ tablespoon flour
⅛ teaspoon salt
   Pinch of pepper
1 teaspoon sugar
¼ cup grated fresh or commercially prepared horseradish
¾ cup cream or half-and-half

In a skillet over medium heat, melt the butter. Add the flour, salt and pepper, sugar, and horseradish. Stir until well blended. Add the cream. Lower heat and cook, stirring constantly, for about 10 minutes or until thick.

Makes 1 cup

Hint: If sauce gets too thick, you can thin with a bit of warm milk.

Another Hint: This is wonderful on everything! I serve it on eggs, steak, fish, chicken, etc.

HOLLANDAISE SAUCE

This is the real thing—a sinful sauce that tastes obscenely delicious. It is not for anyone with a cholesterol problem! Hollandaise has a rotten reputation of being difficult to make. It isn't!

> 12 *egg yolks*
>   *Dash of Tabasco sauce*
> 1 *tablespoon warm water*
> 1 *cup butter, melted*
>   *Juice of ½ lemon*
>   *Pinch of cayenne pepper*

Place the egg yolks in the top half of a double boiler and beat until thick. Add Tabasco and water, beating constantly. Set on the bottom half, over boiling water, and beat until the eggs begin to thicken.

Melt the butter just until warm.

Beating the egg yolks constantly, slowly begin pouring in the warm butter. The sauce will thicken as it gets frothy and lemon-yellow. It should form soft peaks and be a smooth sauce that can't wait to get on your spoon. Add the lemon juice. Keep beating. Add a touch of cayenne to bring out a little more flavor. Don't let the sauce over-heat—if it "breaks" (curdles), you'll have to start all over again: Beat 2 egg yolks in a bowl. Add gradually to the "broken" mixture while constantly beating over a very low flame until thick. Mixture should be warm, *not hot*.

This is traditionally served on eggs Benedict or over fresh vegetables such as steamed asparagus or broccoli.

Makes 2 cups

Hint: If there is any sauce left over, cover and let it sit at room temperature. The next day, beat 2 egg yolks and add to the leftover sauce. Heat in double boiler and beat back to life.

TARRAGON SAUCE

1 *can beef broth*
1 *15-ounce can tomato sauce*
1 *tablespoon flour*
¼ *cup butter*
1 *tablespoon chopped fresh tarragon*

In a saucepan, combine all ingredients and cook, stirring constantly, over medium heat, for 5 minutes or until thick.

Makes 4 cups

Hint: Pour over Ham and Egg Croquettes (see page 68) or cold broccoli.

SALSA

6 *ripe tomatoes, cut into pieces*
4 *hot serrano or jalapeño peppers, fresh or canned (if you want it* really *hot, leave the seeds in; otherwise get rid of them)*
6 *white onions, cut into pieces*
1 *bunch fresh cilantro, washed and trimmed of the roots*
   Pinch of salt
2 *tablespoons cold water*

In the food processor, using the steel blade, blend all ingredients until puréed. This is especially good over enchiladas, tacos, and other Tex-Mex recipes.

Makes 12 servings

Hint: Cover and refrigerate until ready to serve. Salsa keeps, refrigerated, for up to 10 days. Keep it in your Perfect Pantry. You'll find it very useful, as it picks up the taste of so many dishes.

MEXICAN GREEN SAUCE

1 *pound green tomatillos*
1 *serrano pepper*
1 *bunch fresh cilantro, washed and trimmed of roots*
½ *teaspoon white vinegar*
1 *tablespoon chopped onion*

Wash the tomatillos. Peel and cut each one into four sections. In the food processor, using the steel blade, blend them with the pepper, cilantro, vinegar, and onion until puréed. If necessary, add a teaspoon (or two) of water to keep it liquid.

This green sauce can be used with eggs, cold meats, beef, and ham, as well as in soups, Bloody Marys, and Mexican food—in and on anything you choose.

Makes 1½ cups

Hint: Will keep refrigerated, in a covered container, for up to 10 days.

SUPER-EASY TOMATO SAUCE

4 *Italian tomatoes, peeled*
1 *tablespoon plus 1 teaspoon butter or margarine*
1 *teaspoon flour*

In a food processor, using the steel blade, purée the tomatoes. Pour off juice and reserve. In a skillet, over medium heat, melt 1 tablespoon butter or margarine and sauté tomatoes; add about 1 teaspoon of the tomato juice if needed. Blend in the flour and 1 teaspoon butter. Mix, constantly, with a wooden spoon until sauce is thick.

Makes 1 cup

Hint: When melting the butter in the skillet, add a drop of oil. This will prevent butter from burning.

WHITE SAUCE

2 *tablespoons butter or margarine*
2 *tablespoons flour*
1 *cup cream*
  Pinch of salt and pepper
4 *egg yolks, beaten*
4 *tablespoons sherry or white wine*

In a skillet, over low heat, melt the butter or margarine. Stir in the flour until well blended. Add the cream, salt, and pepper and cook, stirring constantly, until thick. When thick, beat in egg yolks and sherry. Serve immediately.

Makes 2 cups

Hint: This basic sauce can be used on so many dishes. I particularly recommend it over my Noodle-Oyster and Clam Loaf (see page 138).

CONDIMENTS

BOYSENBERRY BUTTER WITH HONEY

1 cup butter, softened
1 cup whole boysenberries
⅛ cup honey
Mint for garnish

Combine butter, boysenberries, and honey. Spoon into a small mold. Refrigerate. When firm, turn out of mold. Decorate with mint leaves.

Makes approximately 2 cups

CAJUN SPICE

4 tablespoons paprika
4 tablespoons cayenne pepper
1 teaspoon powdered thyme
1 teaspoon garlic powder
1 teaspoon onion powder
2 tablespoons chili powder
½ teaspoon ground sage

Combine all ingredients. Put into a shaker and place on the table to use on all kinds of foods. This is fiery and hot, but also sweet and flavorful.

Makes approximately ¾ cup

Hint: Keep this on hand with your other herbs and spices. If you like the flavor, experiment with it on all types of foods. It really wakes up many otherwise predictable recipes.

CRANBERRY RELISH

1 *pound fresh cranberries, washed well*
2 *ounces bourbon*
2 *tablespoons brown sugar*
½ *orange, seeded*

Combine the cranberries, bourbon, and brown sugar in the food processor. Using the steel blade, pulsate until everything is chopped fine. Add the orange and chop into the mixture.

Serve immediately or cover and store, refrigerated, for up to 2 weeks.

Makes approximately 2 cups

Hint: Don't make a paste out of this. It is better chunky—so use the "on and off" pulsating technique.

HOMEMADE MAYONNAISE

2 *teaspoons salt*
1 *teaspoon dry mustard*
  Pinch of cayenne pepper or dash of Tabasco
2 *egg yolks*
2 *cups olive oil or safflower oil*
¼ *cup cider vinegar*

Combine dry ingredients in a mixing bowl with the unbeaten yolks. Beat together until thick. While beating, add the oil, dripping it in a stream and beating it in. When the sauce starts to thicken, begin adding vinegar. Alternate the oil and vinegar until everything is blended.

Place in a container, cover tightly, and refrigerate. It will keep for 5 days.

Makes 2½ cups

Hint: Use oil at room temperature.

HOMEMADE ORANGE MARMALADE

The best! Absolutely the best, if I do say so myself. I have been putting this marmalade on the tables at Scully's for years, and it always disappears. Even for those of you who don't like jams and marmalades, I challenge you to make this and then decide.

5 pounds navel oranges
1 cup fresh orange juice
2½ pounds sugar, brown or white

Wash and cut the oranges into ¼-inch-thick slices. Cut the slices into halves and then into quarters. Put them into a large pot and add 1 cup fresh orange juice. Cook on a low flame until tender but still al dente, about 90 minutes. Add the sugar. Mix well and continue cooking. When the sugar has melted and become a caramel syrup, remove from heat. Let cool.

You can keep the marmalade in a covered plastic container in the refrigerator for nearly 2 weeks. You can also freeze it. Serve in tiny, individual dishes to each guest.

It is delicious with tea or coffee, spread on bread, or just plain on a spoon.

Makes 8 pounds of marmalade

Hint: I guarantee that your guests will love my marmalade, just like my customers at Scully's Place. Why not do what I do—give them a small container full of the marmalade to take home. It is a thoughtful gesture, and every bite will remind them of their happy time spent with you.

DESSERTS

ALMOND TART

Bottom and Top Crusts

    1 egg
    1⅔ cups sifted all-purpose flour
    ⅓ cup sugar
    ½ cup sweet butter or margarine
    ½ teaspoon baking powder
    ½ teaspoon salt

Mix all ingredients together in a bowl and knead with your hands until well blended. Let stand for 30 minutes. Divide dough in half and roll out two sheets for the top and bottom crusts. Line a 9-inch pie plate with one sheet of dough. Cut the other sheet into strips to make a lattice top on the tart.

Filling

    ½ cup sugar
    ⅓ cup butter or margarine
    2 eggs
    1 teaspoon vanilla
    ⅔ cup slivered almonds
    ½ teaspoon fresh lemon juice
    2½ tablespoons flour

Preheat oven to 350°.

Beat the sugar and butter until light. Blend in eggs and vanilla. Fold in the almonds, lemon juice, and flour, mixing lightly. Pour the filling into the pie shell. Crisscross top with dough strips to make a lattice. Bake in preheated oven for 35 to 40 minutes or until golden.

Serves 6 to 8

Hint: Spread raspberry jam on the crust before pouring in the almond filling.

CHOCOLATE CHIP COOKIES

¼ cup softened butter or margarine
2 cups brown sugar
¼ cup granulated sugar
2 tablespoons vanilla
3 eggs
½ cup pure maple syrup
½ teaspoon baking soda
½ teaspoon baking powder
1 cup white cake flour
1 12-ounce bag semi-sweet chocolate bits
½ cup chopped walnuts
2 tablespoons butter or margarine for greasing baking sheet

Preheat oven to 350°.

Beat the softened butter for 1 minute. Add the sugars and vanilla and beat until creamy.

In another bowl, beat the eggs for about 1 minute. Add to the sugar with the maple syrup, baking soda, and baking powder. Gradually blend in the flour. Gently stir in the chocolate chips and nuts until well blended.

Generously grease a cookie sheet. A word about cookie size: Maybe it's because I'm a big guy, or maybe it's because I just love to eat, but either way, I like my cookies big! This is how I make them: I scoop out the batter with an ice-cream scoop and drop it on the sheet, pressing down to flatten to about ½-inch thickness with the bottom of a 3-inch glass. I make as many as I can, leaving about 2 inches of space between cookies. Place cookie sheet in preheated oven and bake for 20 minutes. Test by gently touching top of a cookie with a finger—it should be soft to the touch. When done, remove and cool on wire racks. Serve with ice-cold milk or hot coffee or tea.

Makes about 16 cookies

Hint: Don't overcook the cookies and don't keep them in the refrigerator—they'll get hard.

WENDY'S COOKIES

⅓ cup butter
½ cup brown sugar, tightly packed
1 egg
¼ cup currants
1 teaspoon freshly grated lemon rind
1 cup all-purpose flour
1 teaspoon baking powder

Preheat oven to 350°.

In a food processor, using the steel blade, blend the butter until lemon-colored. While the food processor is on, gradually add the brown sugar, a scoop at a time. Add the egg and blend again. Pour the batter out of the processor into a bowl, add the currants and lemon rind, and mix with a wooden spoon.

In another bowl, sift the flour and baking powder. Add the currant mixture to the flour and mix well.

Grease a cookie sheet. Drop the cookie batter a spoonful at a time onto the sheet, leaving about 2 inches between cookies, and bake in the center of the oven for about 10 minutes, or until light brown.

Makes 2 dozen cookies

ULTIMATE CHOCOLATE CAKE

Ruth Bloom taught me how to make this unbelievable chocolate dessert. I've grown to love it so much that I hardly make any others.

Meringue

> 3½ tablespoons unsweetened cocoa powder
> 1 cup confectioner's sugar
> 5 egg whites
> 1 teaspoon vanilla
> ⅔ cup sugar

Preheat oven to 300°. Grease and flour a cookie sheet.

Sift the cocoa powder and confectioner's sugar together. Set aside.

Beat the egg whites and vanilla. While still soft, add 1½ tablespoons sugar. Beat until stiff. At a lower speed, add the remaining sugar. When blended, fold in the cocoa mixture.

Pour the meringue batter into a pastry bag. Using the plain round tip, form three 8- to 10-inch circles on the cookie sheet. Swirl the rest of the meringue batter into the middle of each circle until the circle is solid. (What you are actually doing is creating a swirl motion to form a complete circle of meringue.) Bake at 300° for 1 hour and 5 minutes. Don't let them burn!

Turn the oven off but leave the meringues in to cool. When they are hard, remove from oven and set aside.

Hint: You can make these the day before and store in a sealed plastic bag on the counter. *Never refrigerate a meringue*—it will be ruined.

While the meringue is baking, make the mousse.

Mousse

> 5½ ounces semi-sweet chocolate pieces
> 6½ tablespoons sweet butter, cut into pieces
> 3 egg yolks
> 4 egg whites
> 5 teaspoons sugar
> ½ teaspoon vanilla
> 1 cup heavy cream

Melt the chocolate in the top half of a double boiler over very hot water. Remove from heat and add the butter, a piece at a time, stirring constantly with a wooden spoon. When well mixed, set aside and let cool, about 20 minutes. When cool, stir in the egg yolks one at a time. Mix until well blended.

Beat the egg whites. While still soft, add half the sugar. Beat at lower speed until stiff, then beat in the remaining sugar. Add vanilla. Gradually fold the chocolate mixture into the egg whites. Gently stir until well blended.

Place one meringue on a cake platter. Spread it with a layer of mousse. Top with a layer of meringue, a layer of mousse, and end with the third layer of meringue.

Whip the cream and spread it on the top and sides of the cake.

Serves 10

Hint: This cake sounds rich, and I guess it is, but it tastes wonderful and is especially light. It really doesn't need anything served with it, but you might want to put some chocolate shavings on top for an added touch.

MELODY'S MOM'S GERMAN CARROT CAKE

Melody's mom has been planning to make this cake for our wedding. She's been waiting for six years while I wait for Melody to ask me to marry her. I'll do anything just to get a bite of this cake!

½ cup raisins
1 cup boiling water
  Peel of 1 medium orange
¾ cup granulated sugar
2 cups all-purpose flour
1 tablespoon baking powder
1 tablespoon baking soda
1 teaspoon salt
½ teaspoon ground cinnamon
¼ teaspoon ground nutmeg
¼ teaspoon ground mace
1½ pounds carrots, trimmed and scrubbed
4 eggs
1¼ cups oil
¾ cup light brown sugar, tightly packed
2 tablespoons vanilla
½ cup sour cream
¾ cup walnut halves
4 tablespoons dark rum (optional)

Preheat oven to 350°. Place the oven rack at the lowest possible position.

Place the raisins in a heatproof bowl. Add 1 cup boiling water. Cover and set aside.

In the food processor, using the steel blade, mince the orange peel with ¼ cup granulated sugar. This should take about 1 minute. Clean the container sides with a spatula and process for another minute. Add the remaining sugar, flour, baking powder, baking soda, salt, cinnamon, nutmeg, and mace. Pulse for 5 to 10 seconds to sift together. Pour into another bowl and set aside.

In the food processor using the medium shredding disc, shred the carrots. Transfer shredded carrots to a large mixing bowl.

In the food processor, using the steel blade, blend the eggs, adding the oil a little at a time. When oil is incorporated, blend for an additional 2 minutes. Add the brown sugar, vanilla, sour cream, walnuts, and rum. Blend, stopping and starting, so the batter is well mixed and the nuts coarsely chopped. Add the contents of the food processor to the carrots. Stir until well mixed.

Drain the raisins and stir into the carrot mixture. Gradually add the dry ingredients to the mixture, stirring constantly.

Grease and flour one 10-inch springform pan and fill with batter.

Bake for 1¼ hours in preheated oven or until a knife or a wooden toothpick, when inserted into the middle of the cake, comes out clean. Remove from oven and cool on a wire rack for about 30 minutes. Unmold the cake and cool completely on a wire rack. Frost.

Cream Cheese Frosting for Melody's Mom's German Carrot Cake

¼ cup sweet butter, softened
1½ teaspoons vanilla
1 tablespoon dark rum
1 tablespoon tequila
3 cups confectioner's sugar
2 cups cubed cream cheese, softened
½ cup shredded coconut (optional)

In a food processor, using the steel blade, blend the butter with the vanilla, rum, tequila, and sugar until the sugar is completely absorbed. Clean the sides of the bowl with the spatula and drop the cubes of cream cheese through the food chute. Blend for about 2 minutes or until smooth. Chill for 1 hour. If you want to add coconut, do so after the frosting is chilled.

Spread the frosting on top of the cake and set on the buffet table. Let everyone see how great it looks before you cut it!

Makes 1 10-inch round cake

Hint: Melody's mom sometimes puts a little raspberry jam on the cake before she frosts it.

HONEY CAKE

1 16-ounce jar honey
1 cup hot black coffee
3½ cups sifted all-purpose flour
2 teaspoons baking powder
1 teaspoon baking soda
3 eggs
1 cup sugar
3 tablespoons safflower oil
¼ cup slivered almonds

Preheat oven to 350°.

In a bowl, mix the honey and coffee and let stand for ½ hour. When cool, add all ingredients except almonds. Mix until well blended.

Grease an 8-inch-square glass baking dish. Pour in the batter. Top with almonds laid out in a pretty design. Bake for 1 hour or until a knife inserted in the middle comes out clean.

Remove from the pan and let cool on a wire rack. This cake keeps, refrigerated, for a week or more tightly wrapped in plastic wrap. You can also freeze it.

Makes 1 8-inch honey cake

BREAD AND BUTTER PUDDING

This is a lovely dish for an English-style breakfast.

8 slices of bread, thickly buttered
2 tablespoons sweet butter or margarine
½ cup currants
    Pinch of grated nutmeg
    Grated rind of 1 lemon
3 cups milk
3 eggs
2 tablespoons sugar

Preheat oven to 350°.

Generously butter a 9-inch deep-dish pie plate. Place a layer of thickly buttered bread slices in the bottom and sprinkle with the currants, nutmeg, and lemon rind. Lay down another layer of bread, and continue alternating ingredients until the dish is full or you have finished using the ingredients, whichever comes first.

In a small saucepan over medium heat, bring the milk to a boil. Remove from heat. Beat the eggs and whisk them into the milk. Stir in sugar. Pour over the bread. Place in the oven and bake at 350° for 1 hour or until top is light brown.

Remove from the oven and either let cool for 5 minutes before serving or let stand for an hour and serve at room temperature. Serve with whipped cream or Custard Sauce (see page 165).

Serves 8

Hint: Serve hot with vanilla ice cream.

CHOCOLATE CREAM PUDDING

> *1 small envelope gelatin*
> *4 tablespoons milk*
> *½ cup black coffee*
> *6 ounces unsweetened chocolate, melted*
> *1 tablespoon sugar*
> *2 egg yolks*
> *1 teaspoon vanilla*
> *1 cup heavy cream*
> *1 cup ice cubes*
> *2 packages ladyfingers*
> *Devon Cream (see page 166)*

In the food processor, using the steel blade, mix the gelatin, milk, and coffee. Add the chocolate, sugar, egg yolks, vanilla, and cream. Continue mixing for 30 seconds, then add the ice cubes.

Butter an 8-inch-round glass bowl and line with halves of ladyfingers. Pour the chocolate mixture into the bowl. Cover the top with ladyfingers laid in a sunburst pattern. Chill for at least 4 hours or until set. Serve in individual bowls with Devon cream.

Serves 6 to 8

Hint: Instead of ladyfingers, line the bowl with slices of Honey Cake (see page 182).

CHOCOLATE BREAD PUDDING

1½ to 2 *cups coarse, crouton-size bread crumbs*
   1 *cup semi-sweet chocolate bits, melted*
  ¾ *cup sugar*
   2 *cups milk*
   2 *eggs plus 2 yolks*
   2 *tablespoons sweet butter or margarine*
   1 *teaspoon ground cinnamon*
     Devon Cream (see page 166)

Preheat oven to 350°.

In a medium saucepan over low heat, combine the crumbs, melted chocolate bits, and sugar. Add 1½ cups of milk and cook, stirring constantly, for about 10 minutes or until smooth.

Beat the eggs and yolks with the remaining ½ cup milk. Whisk into the hot mixture. Add the butter and cinnamon and continue cooking until thick.

Grease an 8-inch-square glass baking dish. Pour the pudding into the dish and bake for 20 minutes or until top is light brown. Serve hot or cold with Devon cream.

Serves 6

Hint: Stir a dash of anisette or vanilla into the cream before serving.

CHOCOLATE SOUFFLÉ

  ¼ *cup sweet butter*
  ¼ *cup sifted all-purpose flour*
1½ *ounces unsweetened chocolate, chopped*
   1 *cup milk*
  ¼ *cup sugar*
   3 *egg yolks*
   6 *egg whites*
  ½ *teaspoon confectioner's sugar*
   1 *pint heavy cream for whipping*

Preheat oven to 375°.

In a saucepan over medium heat, melt the butter. Stir in the flour. Blend into a roux with a wooden spoon. Add the chocolate and the milk. Stir in up to ¼ cup of sugar to sweeten. Stir until thick. Add the yolks one at a time and, using a wire whisk, beat until thick and heavy. Remove from heat.

Beat the egg whites until stiff. Fold into the sauce.

Butter and sugar a 6-inch soufflé dish. Pour the mixture into the dish but do not fill it to more than 1 inch from the top. Place in the oven on the middle shelf. Remove the top shelf so the soufflé has room to rise. It will rise the entire time it is in the oven and will come up about 1 inch higher than the soufflé dish. Bake for 40 minutes.

Once you take the soufflé out of the oven it will begin to fall, so have all other dishes ready to serve *before* this is out. Dust with confectioner's sugar.

Serve with whipped cream. (You may want to add ¼ teaspoon vanilla and 1 drop of anisette while you're whipping the cream.)

Serves 2

Variation: Instead of using chocolate, substitute ¼ cup Grand Marnier or ¼ cup puréed raspberries for a Grand Marnier or raspberry soufflé.

Hint: You can make the sauce in advance. Then, while the main course is being served, beat the egg whites, fold them into the sauce, and pour into the prepared soufflé dish. Pop the soufflé into the oven and join your guests for the main course. Remember—you should never let the soufflé wait for you to finish breakfast; *you* should be waiting for the soufflé to come out of the oven. *It must be served immediately—and served hot!*

COFFEE SOUFFLÉ

3 *tablespoons sweet butter*
3 *tablespoons all-purpose flour, sifted*
¾ *cup black coffee*
¼ *cup heavy cream*
5 *eggs, separated*
¼ *cup sugar*
1 *teaspoon vanilla*

Preheat oven to 350°.

Grease a 1½-quart soufflé dish and dust it lightly with sugar. Set aside.

In a small saucepan over medium heat, melt the butter. Add the flour, stirring constantly with a whisk. Cook until smooth. Gradually add the coffee and cream, stirring constantly. Cook until thick.

In the food processor, using the steel blade, beat the egg yolks and sugar until smooth and creamy. Pour in the coffee mixture as you are mixing. Add the vanilla and blend. Pour the mixture into a bowl.

Beat the egg whites until stiff. Fold into the coffee mixture. Pour into the prepared soufflé dish, place in the preheated oven, and bake for 40 to 45 minutes. Remove from oven and serve immediately.

Serves 4 to 6

Hint: You can use yesterday's brewed coffee, or make extra in the morning.

SORBETS

These are wonderful! Any flavor sorbet will give the ultimate final touch to breakfast or brunch. Sorbets are light and gently sweet, with a fruit flavor that is always refreshing. Plus, they are simple to make.

Lime Sorbet

> *1 cup sugar*
> *1 cup water*
> *1 cup fresh lime juice*
> *1 egg white*
> *1 teaspoon freshly grated lime rind*

In a small saucepan, over medium heat, cook the sugar and water, stirring constantly, until the sugar is dissolved. Remove from heat. Cover and chill.

When well-chilled, mix the sugar syrup and lime juice together in a small bowl. Pour into a freezer container, cover, and freeze overnight.

In the morning, put the lime ice into your food processor, add the egg white, and blend well, using the steel blade. Put sorbet back into the freezer container and freeze again until you are ready to serve.

To serve, place a scoop into a stemmed glass and decorate with grated lime rind.

Serves 4

Hint: Never serve sorbet with whipped cream. The cream is too heavy and will kill the refreshing taste. For an added treat, pour a touch of liquor—vodka, gin, rum—into the sorbet mixture before you freeze it. It's a nice surprise to the taste buds!

STRAWBERRY AMOUR

1 *cup chopped fresh strawberries*
½ *teaspoon plus ½ cup sugar*
1 *envelope unflavored gelatin*
2 *eggs, separated*
1¼ *cups milk*
½ *teaspoon vanilla*
  Fresh strawberries for garnish
1 *cup whipped cream*

In a small bowl sprinkle the chopped strawberries with ½ teaspoon sugar. Set aside.

In the top half of a double boiler over very hot water, combine the gelatin and ½ cup sugar. Beat in egg yolks. Add the milk. Using a whisk, beat until the gelatin is dissolved. Remove from heat. Stir in the vanilla and chill in the refrigerator until set.

Beat the egg whites until stiff. Remove the gelatin from the refrigerator and beat until it looks like cream. Fold in the egg whites. Gently mix in the chopped strawberries. Pour into a glass bowl or mold. Refrigerate until you are ready to serve. Garnish with fresh berries and whipped cream.

Serves 6

Hint: Serve with ladyfingers.

MELODY'S ZABAGLIONE

4 *egg yolks*
3 *tablespoons honey*
2 *tablespoons Marsala wine*
  Pinch of ground cinnamon

Beat the egg yolks and honey in the top half of a double boiler, over boiling water, until the mixture is thick and lemon-colored. When thick, place directly over low heat and gradually add the wine, beating constantly until the mixture is the consistency of heavy cream. Quickly stir in the cinnamon.

Serve alone, hot or cold, or as a dessert sauce over any sponge cake, pie, or fresh fruit.

Serves 2 to 3

Hint: If you don't want to use Marsala wine, substitute ½ cup orange juice. It is still delicious and a nice change.

ZABAGLIONE

For a really *late* brunch, try serving this sinful dessert.

> 4 *egg yolks*
> 2 *egg whites*
> 2 *tablespoons Marsala wine or sherry*
> 1 *teaspoon sugar*
>   *Pinch of ground cinnamon*

Beat the egg yolks and whites in the top half of a double boiler, over boiling water, until they become frothy and thick. Do not let them cook! Add the wine, sugar, and cinnamon. Keep beating while the zabaglione continues to thicken.

When really frothing, remove from heat and pour into tall glasses. Champagne glasses are perfect. Sprinkle a little more cinnamon on top and serve immediately.

The taste is fabulous—but this is not a light dessert. Serve it in the winter after a light breakfast.

Serves 2

Hint: Put a dash of brandy in the bottom of the serving glass and swirl it around. Then pour in the zabaglione.

DRINKS

HOT DRINKS
(without alcohol)

GREAT COCOA

Ah! To sit before the fire, hot cocoa in hand, remembering what it was like to be a kid. Even for those of us who prefer being adults, such memories make us smile.

> 4 *heaping teaspoons unsweetened cocoa powder*
> 1 *teaspoon sugar*
> ¼ *teaspoon vanilla*
> 1 *cup water*⎱ *(or leave out water and use 1½ cups milk*
> 1 *cup milk* ⎰ *and ½ cup half-and-half)*
> *Whipped cream or marshmallow, for garnish (optional)*

In a small saucepan over medium heat, bring all ingredients, except garnish, to a slow boil. Remove from heat and top with whipped cream or marshmallow.

Add either:

> 1 *teaspoon Kahlúa*
> 1 *teaspoon instant coffee*

or

> *Pinch of ground cinnamon and/or nutmeg*

Serves 1

Hint: I prefer using imported cocoa, from either Holland, England, or Switzerland.

CAFÉ AU LAIT

½ cup freshly brewed hot coffee
½ cup hot steaming milk

Into a cup, pour—at the same time—hot coffee and the steaming milk.

Serves 1

COLD DRINKS
(without alcohol)

ICED CINNAMON COFFEE

> 6 *cups freshly brewed coffee*
> ½ *teaspoon ground cloves*
> 4 *cinnamon sticks*
> 2 *tablespoons sugar*
> ½ *cup vanilla ice cream*
> 6 *tablespoons whipped cream, for garnish (optional)*
> 4 to 6 *chocolate coffee beans, for garnish (optional)*

While the coffee is still in the coffee pot, add the spices. Cover and let sit for an hour.

Remove the cinnamon sticks and pour the coffee into the blender. Add the sugar and vanilla ice cream and blend until thick. Serve in tall iced-tea glasses (I sometimes use champagne flutes) and top with whipped cream if desired.

Serves 4 to 6

Hint: For an added touch, garnish the top of each glass with a chocolate coffee bean.

ICED COFFEE

> 6 *cups freshly brewed coffee, cooled*
> 2 *cups half-and-half*
> 1 *tablespoon vanilla*
> ½ *cup coffee ice cream, softened*

Pour all ingredients into the food processor or blender and whip. Pour into tall glasses and serve immediately or chill until ready to serve.

Serves 4

Hint: Drink through straws.

SCULLY'S ICED TEA

8 cups English Breakfast, Royal Blend, or Darjeeling tea
1 quart ice cubes
1 orange, sliced
1 lemon, sliced

Brew tea as strong as you like it. Let cool for 15 minutes. Pour into a large pitcher and add lots of ice.

Add the orange and lemon slices to the pitcher and let stand for 5 to 10 minutes.

Pour into tall, chilled glasses and serve with an additional slice of lemon and orange in each glass.

Serves 4 to 6

Hint: If you like mint, add fresh mint leaves to each glass. You may also want to add a shot of Lemon Hart Rum.

SILVER FIZZ

4 egg whites
8 tablespoons fresh lemon juice
3 tablespoons sugar
2 cups shaved ice
1 bottle carbonated soda water
Lemon peel, for garnish
4 maraschino cherries

Whip the egg whites, lemon juice, sugar, and ice together in the blender. Fill tall glasses to 1½ inches from the top. Fill to top with carbonated water. Garnish with lemon peel and cherry.

Serves 4

Hint: Don't forget to add 1 shot Beefeater gin per serving for the rowdier bunch.

EGGNOG

4 eggs, beaten
4 tablespoons sugar or honey
3 cups milk
¼ cup pure vanilla
  Pinch of grated nutmeg
1 tablespoon rum or brandy (optional)

Combine the eggs and sugar or honey. Whisk until sugar is dissolved. Stir in the milk and vanilla. Pour into tall glasses. Sprinkle nutmeg on the top and serve cold. If you like, you can add the rum or brandy, mix in the food processor, and then serve.

Serves 4

Hint: Serve in stemmed glasses rather than in cups. I swear it tastes better!

HOT DRINKS
(with alcohol)

CALYPSO COFFEE

1 cup freshly brewed hot coffee
1 cinnamon stick
1 tablespoon rum
½ teaspoon Cointreau
½ teaspoon Kahlúa
1 tablespoon whipped cream
  Pinch of ground cinnamon

Add a cinnamon stick, Barbados or Myers rum, Cointreau and Kahlúa to 1 cup hot brewed coffee. Garnish with whipped cream. Sprinkle with cinnamon. Serve in a mug.

Serves 1

Hint: Use the cinnamon stick as a stirrer.

COFFEE BRÛLÉ

1 cup freshly brewed coffee
1 ounce brandy
2 tablespoons whipped cream
1 teaspoon brown sugar

Preheat oven to Broil.

Into a mug of hot coffee, pour 1 ounce brandy. Spoon whipped cream on top and sprinkle with brown sugar. Put the mug under the broiler so that the sugar will crystallize. Remove from heat and serve immediately.

Serves 1

Hint: Use espresso coffee for extra flavor.

FIREPLACE COFFEE

I once dated a woman who insisted on serving this coffee every time we sat in front of her fireplace. I never complained—I liked her and I loved the coffee.

> 8 *cups freshly brewed coffee*
> 4 *cinnamon sticks*
> 1 *tablespoon freshly grated orange rind*
> 1 *tablespoon freshly grated lemon rind*
> 1 *tablespoon chocolate syrup*
> 2 *tablespoons chocolate liqueur*
> 8 *tablespoons whipped cream*
> 6 to 8 *coffee beans, for garnish (optional)*
> 2 *tablespoons fresh chocolate shavings, for garnish (optional)*

In a medium saucepan, over *very low heat*, mix together the coffee, cinnamon sticks, orange and lemon rind, chocolate syrup, and chocolate liqueur. Simmer for 15 minutes. *Don't let it boil or burn.* Strain into coffee mugs or cups. Put 1 tablespoon whipped cream on top, garnish with a coffee bean or fresh chocolate shavings, and serve immediately.

Makes 6 to 8 cups

IRISH COFFEE

> 1 *cup freshly brewed strong coffee*
> 1 *sugar lump*
> 1 *ounce Murphy's Irish Whiskey*
> 1 *tablespoon whipped cream*
> *Pinch of ground cinnamon*

Pour the coffee into a large mug. Add a lump of sugar and 1 ounce whiskey. Stir. Top with a tablespoon of whipped cream, sprinkle with cinnamon, and serve.

Serves 1

Hint: Always drink the coffee "through" the cream. Don't stir the two together.

COLD DRINKS
(with alcohol)

BLACK VELVET

½ cup champagne
½ cup Guinness Stout

Combine, in equal parts, champagne and stout. Serve immediately in a champagne glass.

Serves 1

BLOODY TEQUILA MARY

2 ounces tequila
2 ounces Mexican Green Sauce (see page 170)
12 ounces tomato juice
Crushed ice
2 celery sticks

Mix together the tequila, green sauce, and tomato juice. Divide equally between two tall glasses. Add crushed ice. Garnish each with celery stick.

Serves 2

Hint: You can also use tomato and clam juice (Clamato) instead of tomato juice.

CHAMPAGNE PUNCH

1 quart cold champagne
½ cup brandy
1 fifth sauterne, cold
1 quart ice
1 orange, sliced thin

Mix together the champagne, brandy, and sauterne wine. Pour over ice into tall champagne glasses and garnish with orange slices.

Serves 8

LONG TAIL

Don't ask me where it got its name. All I remember is drinking it often in Bermuda.

6 ounces light white rum
2 ounces fresh lemon juice
2 ounces Triple Sec
1 ounce Parfait Amour
1 ounce grenadine
1 teaspoon superfine or bar sugar

Place all ingredients into a cocktail shaker. Shake well. Pour over crushed ice into tall glasses. Serve immediately.

Serves 4

Hint: Decorate the glasses with slices of pineapple.

SANGRIA

An old favorite and it's still a hit! I keep a fresh pitcher of it in the restaurant at all times.

> 1 *lemon, seeded and sliced*
> 1 *lime, seeded and sliced*
> 1 *orange, seeded and sliced*
> ¼ *cup brandy*
> ¼ *cup sugar*
> 1 *bottle Spanish red wine*
> 2 *tablespoons fresh lemon juice*
> *Ice cubes*
> *Carbonated water*

Put the fruit slices in a large pitcher. Add the brandy and the sugar. Stir to blend. Let stand at room temperature for 1 hour.

Add the red wine and lemon juice. Stir thoroughly. Let stand at room temperature for another hour.

Just before serving, add ice cubes and carbonated water. Stir briskly; serve in chilled glasses. Garnish each glass with a slice of orange or a fresh strawberry. Enjoy!

Serves 2 or 3

Hint: Sometimes I serve sangria before breakfast, sometimes after. It's also great when watching football. Don't make the mistake of saving this drink just for Mexican breakfasts—enjoy it often. But don't overdo it, especially if your guests are driving home. A little sangria goes a long way!

STRAWBERRY WINE DAIQUIRI

1 *quart ice cubes*
1 *cup sliced fresh (or unsweetened frozen) strawberries*
  Juice of 2 limes
1 *cup white wine*
¼ *cup strawberry Jell-O powder*

Place the ice cubes in the blender. Crush and pour off the water. Add berries, lime juice, wine (a Chablis will do nicely), and the Jell-O powder. Process to mix well.

Serve in tall glasses with a long spoon. You can garnish with a berry dipped in confectioner's sugar if you like.

Serves 4

Hint: Serve before breakfast—it's mild and mellow.

THE
PERFECT
PANTRY

BACON

Keep frozen

BATTERS

Pancake and/or waffle
refrigerated: tightly covered, 3 days
frozen: tightly covered, 3 months

BREAD

Freeze your favorite
A variety of your favorite crackers
Breadsticks
Biscuits
Homemade bread crumbs—
keep refrigerated

CEREALS

Cream of Wheat
Dry, any kind you like
Oatmeal

CHEESES

Any and all that you can't live without

CHOCOLATE

Squares for baking and cooking
Chips for baking
Cocoa powder

COFFEE

Beans
Instant
Decaffeinated, beans and instant

EGGS

One dozen at a time, otherwise they will not be fresh

FISH

Canned—tuna, sardines, anchovies, salmon

FLOUR

All-purpose
Cake flour
Whole-wheat flour
Matzo meal

FRUIT

Apples
Oranges
Limes
Lemons

FRUITS, DRIED

Raisins, apricots, prunes, and any others you like

GARLIC

Keep dried or powdered in a jar on the shelf with your spices, but always keep fresh cloves on hand as well

JAM

Any flavors you like; once you open a jar, put it in the refrigerator

JUICE

Fruit—assorted, plain, and combined

Frozen orange, grapefruit,
and pineapple
Canned tomato and Cla-
mato

MILK
Nonfat
Nonfat plain yogurt
Any flavor yogurt
Whipping cream
Half-and-half

MUSTARD
Dijon
Peppercorn
Any other fancy mustard

NUTS
Almonds, whole and sliv-
ered
Peanuts
Sesame seeds

OILS
Vegetable
Peanut
Olive

ONIONS
White
Shallots
Chives

PASTA
Spaghetti
Vermicelli
Any macaroni in any shape

POTATOES
Baking
Red

POWDERS
Baking powder
Baking soda
Cornstarch

RICE
White
Brown
Wild

SAUCES
Tabasco
Worcestershire

SOUPS
Canned chicken and beef
broth. In an emergency,
they make good stock
bases. You can also use
chicken stock to replace
water in rice recipes.

SPICES
Every one you are accus-
tomed to using, plus some
exotic ones just in case.
A good selection is essential for cooking. This includes beef and chicken
bouillon cubes, bouquet
garni, spaghetti season-
ing, lemon and orange
peels, and the like. Keep
the jars alphabetized for
easy use in a drawer or in
your pantry. Especially
Scully's Cajun Spice,
which you make yourself
(see page 172).

SUGAR
Granulated
Confectioner's
Brown

SYRUP
Maple
Boysenberry or strawberry
Honey

TEA
> Loose
> Bags
> Herb tea in bags

VANILLA

VEGETABLES, CANNED
> Italian tomatoes, whole
> Tomato sauce and tomato paste
> Olives (I prefer them in jars)—black, Greek, and Italian; large green

Capers (again, in jars)
Beans—pinto, kidney, and cannellini
Artichoke hearts

VEGETABLES, FROZEN
> Chopped spinach
> Chopped broccoli
> Artichoke hearts

VINEGARS
> White
> Red wine
> Any other exotic flavor you like

THE PERFECTLY PREPARED KITCHEN

2 sets measuring cups
1 set measuring spoons
Cutting board
Grater
Sifter
Funnel
1 metal spatula
3 rubber spatulas
3 to 4 wooden spoons, different sizes
Slotted metal spoon
2 wire whisks
2 6-inch Teflon frying pans
2 9½-inch cast-iron frying pans
1 3-quart pot
1 2-quart pot
1 1-quart pot
Deep fryer
Double boiler
Electric mixer (hand-held)
Food processor
1 chopping knife
1 serrated knife, long
1 12-inch chef's knife
1 paring knife
1 6-inch utility knife
1 or 2 sets metal or ceramic mixing bowls
Meat thermometer
Timer
Knife sharpener
Vegetable peeler
Can opener
Bottle opener

Slotted spoon
Soup ladle
Garlic press
Colander
Strainer (stainless steel)
Vegetable steamer
Plastic baster
Kitchen scissors
2 pastry brushes
Tongs
Tea kettle
Coffeepot
Free-standing plastic chopping board
Salad drier
Pie pans
Cookie sheet
Tart pan
Bundt pan
8-inch square pan
12-cup muffin pan
Popover pan
2 9-inch round cake pans
2 9 × 5-inch loaf pans
2-quart soufflé dish
6 to 8 4-inch soufflé dishes
Rolling pin
Crepe pan (non-stick or cast iron)
2 5¾ × 3-inch mini loaf pans
Doughnut cutter
Stockpot
Glass baking dish
Waffle iron

INDEX